A Questionable Serial Killer

Herman Payne

Published by Trellis Publishing, 2021.

A QUESTIONABLE SERIAL KILLER

First edition. July 11, 2021.

Copyright © 2021 Herman Payne.

ISBN: 979-8224789030

Written by Herman Payne.

A QUESTIONABLE SERIAL KILLER

HERMAN PAYNE

Confessions Of A Questionable Serial Killer

Robert Charles Browne, a 68-year old Louisiana native, who serves a double-life sentence at the Colorado Territorial Correctional Facility may just be one of the most prolific murderers in American history. However, some of the self-professed serial killer's uncorroborated claims leaves plenty of room for speculation about the cold cases that remain unsolved in the wake of his imprisonment.

Born October 31, 1952, Browne grew up in Coushatta, Louisiana as the youngest of nine children. In many news articles that followed his arrest in Colorado Springs, Browne's hassles with authority were made public knowledge and it became a known fact that in 1969, at the age of 17, he dropped out of high school to join the Army. Browne did one tour in Vietnam and another in South Korea, but was dishonorably discharged for drug abuse from the latter.

The story unfolds as Browne returns to the United States where he worked a number of odd jobs at a wholesale store, at a paper company in Louisiana, and was employed as a delivery man at a flower shop in Texas before he handled a kwik-shop counter in Colorado Springs during 1987.

Apart from his colorful resume, Browne found himself in front of the altar five times and it is said that all of his wives were small-boned, demure in nature and no more than five feet tall.

Much later on, when the dust began to settle on the files of the unresolved murders he claimed to be responsible for, his fourth wife managed to speak out against her former husband's disdain for women and the authorities.

She also told *The Colorado Springs Gazette* that Browne had put a pistol to her head and managed to pull the trigger, but when nothing happened, he handed over the gun and asked her to shoot him instead.

This revelation spurred Browne's third wife to sit down for an interview, in which she detailed how she was beaten because she forgot to put a serving spoon in his gravy and then politely asked authorities to call her when they 'pulled the switch.'

The alleged serial killer's first brush with the law took place in 1986 when he was jailed for car-theft in Louisiana. A history of arson, cruelty to animals, and burglary was exposed during his court hearing, which only supported the theory that Browne's troubled past was a fair indication of the things that he was capable of.

Shortly after his early release from jail in Louisiana, Browne moved to Colorado where things altogether took a turn for the worse. In his first court appearance (following his El Paso County arrest in March 1995) he bluntly confessed to murdering 49 people during several interrogations.

At the time of the arrest, County Sheriff Terry Maketa felt that Browne's claims were credible adding that Browne may be exaggerating, but didn't think that the authorities can 'conduct this kind of business assuming that he is.' Maketa and the El Paso County Police Department investigators continued to follow leads well after Browne's confinement.

Browne's childhood in an impoverished family was calamitous, and the chronicles of his life have been documented in a fashion that suggests an unequivocal lack of empathy from a young age. His life story may be perfect for a tragic biopic along the lines of 2004's *Monster*, but make no mistake - Robert Browne is no Aileen Wuornos. His motives for murder had nothing to do with revenge, and thanks to his fickle homicidal methods, investigators were unable to link a long list of crimes to him at first.

True Traces

The death of Heather Dawn Church on Rampart Range Road, northwest of Colorado Springs, and the September 16 discovery of her remains in 1993, had the authorities piecing together the horrific details of the homicide for months on end.

Two years after the vanishing of Church, her skull was discovered on the slopes of a hill near Rampart Range Road; about 30 miles from her parents' house in Black Forest at the time. Initially, Micheal Church (Heather's father) was the considered to be the prime suspect, but by the time the murder case was televised on *America's Most Wanted*, a set of fingerprints were discovered on the frame of a window screen and was deemed the only hopeful key forensic evidence the Colorado authorities had.

Unfortunately, The Colorado Bureau of Investigation and the FBI were unable to determine a match for the fingerprints at first. Back then, fingerprint data banks had no server or system in place that connected them.

Enter Thomas Carney - A Colorado county fingerprint specialist, who was asked by the Colorado Bureau of Investigation to prepare 8-by-10-inch photographs of the fingerprints which were mailed to all of the 52 jurisdictions. The images were run against the computerized systems of each data bank, and by March 1995, their efforts had paid off.

The Colorado authorities determined that the fingerprints of the suspect in question was a hazel-eyed white male, 6 feet 2 inches in height, weighed roughly 180 pounds, and had a Southern accent.

The very same man was formerly convicted of vehicle theft and burglary in Louisiana, but the winning indication pointed the authorities to the location of a mobile home in Colorado Springs where the suspect was said to be living at the time - only half-a-mile down the road from Heather Church's house.

The man in question?

Robert Charles Browne.

The Full Confessional

At first, Browne claimed to know nothing about Heather's vanishing after county search-and-rescue personnel raided his trailer home. FBI agents canvassed the neighborhood and questioned residents in the area to gather as much information as possible about Browne's involvement within the community. His house had been previously bypassed because it was outside of their perimeter search.

Four years after the murder, Browne was brought in for a videotape interview and the El Paso County detectives were trying to piece the fateful event together that took the life of Heather Church.

Did he ever set foot on the property of the Church family before the disappearance of their daughter? Did he drop by to clean out a gutter or to complete a construction task?

Browne firmly responded with a "no" and said that he had never been there in his life.

Detective Mark A. Finley, who was conducting the interview that day, looked Browne in the eyes and told him that his fingerprints matched those that were found on the window screen of the Church house. The now-convicted killer then cheekily suggested that they run the prints again.

The fingerprints were a 100% match, but that was the only evidence they had that linked him to this specific crime. Much to the surprise of law-enforcement officials, Browne quickly changed his tune by confessing to the murder of Heather Church on the spot.

In detail, he later admitted to a placement counselor that he caught Heather off guard and killed her in the house of her parents by breaking her neck.

In June 2006, Browne also plead guilty to the first-degree murder of Rocio Delpilar Sperry, who was found dead on November 1987 at the age of 15, inside a Colorado Springs apartment complex.

It was a confusing affair, to say the least.

On one hand, Browne went on record to confess, but pleaded not guilty to the charges in court. Eventually, Browne probably saw what was coming his way and sought a plea agreement (to avoid the death penalty) and was once again found guilty of two first-degree murders in the Fourth Judicial District Court based on the new terms of his incarceration.

Curiously, Browne's churlishness with the police's inefficacy in linking his involvement with the murders grew substantially while he was in prison. But one has to wonder: Did this man's plea bargain become part of a greater plan to share the details of the murders he claimed to be responsible for?

Between exchanges of taunting letters and sporadic meetings Browne had with El Paso's cold-case department volunteering investigator Charlie Hess, it became clear that there was a method to his madness after all. From the start, Browne wanted to make it clear who was in charge of the narrative that lasted around four years and was said to often break off communications abruptly.

Hess later claimed that Browne did not want other investigators to see him in person. This agreement was short-lived until he stopped all communication again before finally allowing investigators to become a part of the conversation. "Little by little he gave us bits of information," observed Hess. "Being non-judgemental was necessary."

With each session, Browne brought terms of negotiations to the table that mostly included requests for special treatment. Hess stated that Browne only shared information about two or three murders each time; keeping the investigators right where he wanted to. However, "all of the things he asked for were reasonable, within the law and the rules of the DOC." according to Hess.

Ultimately Unresolved

Browne's first murder is said to date back to 1970 in South Korea, and apart from the two killings he was found guilty of, he claimed to have strangled, shot, and stabbed an additional 47 men and women at random roadside turnouts, alleys, and bars.

El Paso's cold-case department investigator Charlie Hess was convinced that there were more grizzly details to uncover, and at one point told reporters that it became obvious that they 'had to go on.'

Hess's gut feeling had much to do with his work as a former FBI and CIA agent, which led to his involvement in volunteering at the sheriff's office to investigate and possibly solve cold cases. Hess mentioned that the El Paso police force preferred not to use the term cold cases. "We like to call them unresolved cases. A cold case would indicate that a case is put on the shelf and forgotten. We don't forget them," he said.

As Browne's claims piled up over the years, the El Paso authorities had no choice but to report all possible homicides - despite widespread skepticism in the media. The unresolved cases have remained a mystery until now and no bodies have been discovered that may suggest the authenticity of all the claims that were recorded.

The sheriff's department stated that only six of Browne's confessions were detailed enough to be linked tentatively to some of the unsolved crimes.

The collective testimonials of Robert Browne would later elucidate information of one victim in South Korea, seven in Texas, nine in Colorado, 17 in Louisiana, three in Mississippi, five in Arkansas, two in California, Oklahoma, and New Mexico, and one more victim in the state of Washington.

The Browne Fine-Print

All things considered, if Browne's testimonies are to be considered valid, his crimes would account for a grim guidebook on a variety of ways in which to kill.

Browne confidently claimed to have shot some of his victims in cold blood, while others were strangled or viciously stabbed. He described an incident where he smothered a female victim with a pesticide-soaked rag before stabbing her nearly 30 times with a screwdriver. He also recounted his steps as he fatally wounded another victim with an ice pick after knocking her out with ether.

"Sometimes killers do not replicate things from one crime to the next," criminologist Robert Keppel observed. The Sam Houston State professor and author of the 1997 book Signature Killers also felt that Browne's particular modus operandi made things more complicated for the police.

As for the rest of the unsupported attestations, investigators were unable to confirm if there were any bodies found on the long list of victims that succumbed at the hands of Browne. Conveniently, there were cases he claimed to not remember enough details of to assist investigators in pursuing these homicidal cases to the very end.

With the help of court papers, the media was able to present a predator to the world - A man who despised women and felt like they were deserving of his wrath because they were unfaithful. The irony in these claims is that most of these women cheated on their boyfriends and husbands with him.

The fine-print of Robert Browne's killing sprees doesn't illustrate a methodical killer, nor a vengeful one. His motive to kill sprung from disappointment and the disrespect he had for women. "They are untrue, they sleep around a lot, they cheat and they are not of the highest moral value," Browne told investigators who were struggling to piece together a wild goose chase brimming with partially-substantial evidence.

In contrast to all of this, Browne admitted that he rarely ever planned a killing, but instead went out to search for his prey at random. Mostly everyday settings applied and made it 'easier' for him to execute his murderous plans, but it was the descriptions of these random killings that made these crimes so unspeakably cruel.

It became obvious that the authorities had a relentless murderer on their hands. During the prison interviews that were conducted, Browne claimed that he relied on a random impulse and when the opportunity was there, he would jump at it because "it was just disgust with the person and some of it just confrontation." he remarked.

These statements brought Sheriff Maketa to the conclusion that Browne initially got away with his crimes because he never bothered spying on his victims, or by surveilling them. He didn't spend any time with them before he killed either.

What really shook Sheriff Maketa was Browne's innate ability to dispose of his victims' bodies with such ease and impenitence.

Close Contact

Following the incarceration of Robert Browne, Mike Church was able to find some closure, but when he came to know about the claims of an additional 48 murders that took place, he felt an overwhelming flood of emotions like he did the first time.

"He's sick. He's sadistic and I feel that he is a coward," Church told a local Colorado Springs newspaper.

"There seems to be no closure for me, this is the second time he's come around."

All things considered, Browne was found guilty of only two first-degree murders and then thought it necessary to protect his own life by asking to be moved to a different prison system. Tragically, the remaining families of Browne's victims may never find closure either.

"You never give up hope, you're always waiting for a phone call, you're always waiting for a knock at your door." Church mentioned.

He then went on to say that he hopes "Browne dies in prison."

Browne's childhood gym class teacher in Coushatta, Johnny Norman, was convinced that the convicted killer's unrepentant nature is a product of his damaged upbringing. He noted Browne as a 'smart kid with a bad temper' and recalled a basketball game where someone fouled him and 'flew off the handle in fury.'

Retired Colorado Springs police investigator Lou Smit worked closely alongside Terry Maketa and Charlie Hess to build the Church case. This is also the man who is famous for suggesting that JonBenet

Ramsey's killer was an intruder, and the person who had a gut feeling that Browne was even worse than the actual picture he portrayed in interviews and interrogations.

Browne, who is said to have an IQ of 140, expertly executed every killing he is responsible for, and Norman (who later became a parish sheriff) also added that "You just don't think in a small community like Colorado Springs someone would do something like that and be from a place like Coushatta."

Another person who tried to understand the inner-workings of Browne's mind, Sheriff Terry Maketa considered Browne to be 'highly intelligent and felt that he 'knew exactly what he was doing.'

The Man Of The Hour

When he stepped off the cold case circuit as the de facto advisor and volunteer for the El Paso Police Department, Charlie Hess looked back at that whirlwind of an experience and told

The New York Times that "Why?" no longer mattered to him.

He spent a good portion of his life weaving through the minds of criminals at the FBI and extracting secrets as a CIA agent in Vietnam, but nothing really exasperated him as much as The Robert Charles Browne Case in which he played a pivotal part.

Hess' interview with *The New York Times* was illuminating. It contained behind-the-scenes details that interested, invested and affected parties wanted to read. Apart from sticking to the facts, the retired FBI agent made it his mission to establish names, dates, locations, cause and manner of death to an extraordinary extent. If there was one person Robert Browne may have feared, the arrow would point to Charlie Hess.

He remembers the integrations with Browne like it was yesterday. At first, he was convinced that the questions he was asking was enough to work this man, who by his own account, killed 49 people, into a confessional corner. But Hess soon realized that "Why?" didn't close cases.

It was becoming a useless tactic that didn't resonate with Browne one bit.

Even if Browne was considered to be hyper-intelligent, the "Why?" question is something that is reserved for intellectuals. Browne, on the other hand, was someone who simply got things done because he was smart.

When Hess began his volunteering at the El Paso Police Department's cold case department, he rummaged through files that no-one had looked at in decades. One case in particular stood out and before he knew it, an exchange of letters between Hess and Browne developed into a relationship that was largely based on trust and reciprocation.

On the back-burner, Hess tracked down names, devoured missing people's reports and conducted hundreds of interviews. He made trips to the penitentiary where Browne was imprisoned and quite often, he wondered what the purpose of it all was.

On a number of occasions, Hess had quit, but always found himself back at the desk where eventually, months became years. But deep down he was thinking of the things he could've been doing instead.

Like fishing. Spending time with his family. Walking the dogs.

Working on a case of this magnitude presented its side-effects in a variety of ways and what Hess remembers vividly is the constant lack of appetite. He could barely eat after a day of extracting vital information from a man who really just wanted to sleep on a better prison mattress.

Night after night Hess wondered why he was spending so much time with someone who was already locked away for life with no hope of parole on the horizon. He reached a point where he found himself running into walls at every turn and decided to hang up his hat for good.

When Hess left the El Paso Police Department, things didn't end well as one may think. The Bureau Chief demanded that Hess sign a confidentiality report which he saw as a slap in the face. Especially whe

Hess claimed that he had never given them any reason not to trust him with sensitive information.

Before walking out, Hess received the Sheriff's Meritorious Service Award which was probably the best way to close a chapter, and to flip the proverbial bird to those in question. A few years later, Hess took matters into his own hands when he co-authored a book titled *Hello, Charlie: Letters From A Serial Killer* - A riveting account of Hess' unprecedented correspondence with Robert Charles Browne.

In the book, Hess asked himself "Why?" one last time, and he acknowledges the driving force that was there all along. He knew all too well what it meant to lose someone at the hands of a murderer. It served as an influential tonic in the work he did with Browne, but it was the only thing that was able to ultimately draw him from that dark place he considered eternal.

Katherine Hayes, 15, was reported missing July 4, 1980, in Louisiana. Hayes' body was found Oct. 16, 1980, in Nantachie Creek. She had been strangled.

Wanda Faye Hudson, 21, was found dead on May 28, 1983, in her Coushatta, La., apartment. She had been stabbed multiple times. Coushatta is Browne's hometown. Browne had done maintenance work on Hudson's apartment, including changing the lock on her door.

Faye Self, 26, was reported missing March 30, 1983, in Louisiana. Browne told authorities that her body was dumped in the Red River. She has never been found.

Melody Bush, 22, was found dead on March 30, 1984, in Fayette County, Texas. Her body was found in a drainage ditch and the coroner ruled Bush died of acute acetone poisoning.

Nidia Mendoza, 17, was reported missing on Feb. 2, 1984, in Texas. Her body was found on Feb. 6, 1984, in a ditch.

Rocio Sperry, 15, was reported missing on Nov. 15, 1987, in El Paso County. Browne, who pleaded guilty Thursday and was sentenced to life in prison in this case, told an investigator that he dumped Sperry's body in a trash bin after strangling her in his apartment. Sperry has never been found.

Heather Dawn Church, 13, was reported missing on Sept. 17, 1991, in El Paso County. Church's remains were found on Sept. 16, 1993, on Rampart Range Road northwest of Colorado Springs. Browne is serving a life sentence in her death.

Lisa Lowe, 21, was reported missing on Nov. 3, 1991, in Arkansas. Lowe's body was found on Nov. 26, 1991, in the St. Francis River.

BETTY LOU WILL KILL YOU

ALICE WILSON

Betty Lou Beets is a perfect historical example of how multifaceted crime can be, how a victim could become an aggressor, or an aggressor may adopt the mask of victimhood, and how all is not necessarily as it seems. Convicted for murdering two men and assaulting or attempting to kill four, Betty Lou's story is one that would send chills down the spine of any man from any era. Only the fourth woman to be executed for murder, despite the overall statistics hovering around forty to fifty cases of capital punishment per year, her crimes were too gruesome and cold for the court to offer her a lesser sentence... or were they? As we shall see when we delve into her history, despite Betty Lou's extensive criminal record and constant charges against her from ex husbands and her own children, the justice system was eager to give her a way out of the death sentence and allow her to live her natural life out in prison. And although there were some mitigating circumstances, it is telling that Betty Lou Beets almost got away with a life sentence in a situation where many others would have been executed without remorse.

Betty Lou Beets was born Betty Lou Dunevant on the 12th of March 1937, in Roxboro, North Carolina, USA. Her parents were initially tobacco farmers, whose main pleasure in life was alcohol, resulting in rampant alcoholism and a violent family life not atypical of the rural poor of the Great Depression. They lived on a diet of salt pork and various flours, barely touching vegetables or fruit, let alone eggs, fish, nuts or pulses, essential for developing a healthy brain and body. Furthermore, Betty Lou was disabled. She was not completely deaf, but hard of hearing due to having contracted the measles some time between the ages of three and six. Her fever was so severe and prolonged that she suffered damage to her brain and ears. As her hearing was affected at such a young age, she suffered an impairment to her speech similar to what many deaf or hard of hearing children suffer. At another time, or in another family, Betty Lou may have received treatment and hearing aids, but as a poor family in 1940, they could not afford to get her the treatment she would have needed to hear and speak normally. Her education was strongly impacted as she could not learn to read or study, resulting in borderline illiteracy and innumeracy and a frustrating life at home and away. Betty Lou also claimed she had been raped by her father in early childhood, as well as sexually abused by others. By the age of twelve her family life was falling apart. Her mother had been institutionalized due to breakdowns caused by alcoholism and Betty Lou had to drop out of school so she could care for her younger brother and sister. Her father, who seemed to see her as a surrogate mother for her siblings, became guarded against any sign of Betty Lou escaping and would beat her for not taking full responsibility for her siblings. She was often at the doctor's office or in hospital for the injuries he inflicted on her. She finally left school completely. The family moved to Hampton, Virginia, while Betty Lou was still a young girl, so that her father could work as a machinist. They were poor, she was young and disabled and she was a victim at the hands of the very people who were supposed to care for her. These circumstances were hardly the healthiest for the young girl to grow up in, and it is not shocking that Betty Lou became increasingly unstable and inclined to criminality in such an environment during such a time of deprivation. However it is also noteworthy that many more people suffered equal or worse hardship, yet did not turn to criminal activity. Perhaps it was the combination of everything, all together at once, but as she grew up something was going very, very wrong inside Betty Lou.

At the age of fifteen she married her first husband, Robert Franklin Branson. Far from an age where anyone feels quite ready to move into adulthood, Betty Lou was married for the first time. She would remain with him for seventeen years before finally divorcing. Although she levied accusations of violence against all her husbands, Robert Franklin Branson was the only one whose life she did not threaten directly herself. It appears he picked up where her father left off. If she was ever a unilateral victim, this may have been the one time. Within the first year she attempted suicide and became pregnant. They had a daughter together. She also later had a son with Robert Branson, who was also named Robert after his father. They went onto have four more children. Their children may have been a factor in reducing the marital violence, extending the duration of the relationship and, ultimately, saving Robert Branson Senior's life. In 1958 he evicted her from their home and put her on a bus to Virginia while he kept her children, at which point Betty again attempted suicide via an overdose of sleeping pills. They divorced in 1969, which left Betty Lou a financial and emotional wreck.

Being single took its toll on Betty Lou. She attached her self-worth to her ability to stay married. She began drinking to fight her feelings of loneliness. Between her own insecurities and the hard time she had getting money from either Robert Branson or the Welfare service to support her, Betty Lou soon felt she needed to remarry. She married Billy York Lane at the age of thirty two. Their marriage was a tumultuous one, and very short. There was evidence of mutual violence and disregard for each other's wellbeing. Lane had been abusive towards a previous partner and Betty Lou responded to his violence in turn. Her daughters recall how he used to beat her senseless and how she used to attack him. He initially wanted to charge her for attempted murder, but swiftly dropped the charges after he was forced to admit he had attacked her, broken her nose and threatened her life. They divorced the same year and remarried again shortly after the trial. After Betty Lou shot at him, Billy York Lane divorced her again, only a month after their remarriage, this time for good. It would prove the wisest decision of his life, as her subsequent husbands found out.

Betty Lou remained single for a year and unmarried for eight more years. During the interim Betty Lou worked in a warehouse, then took up work at a topless bar to cover the bills. She sent two of their children back home to Branson, as she could not afford to care for them. She went on to marry Ronnie C. Threlkold, her boyfriend of seven years, at the age of forty. However this relationship would be as unpredictable, violent and dangerous for Ronnie as it was for Billy. In this case there was little evidence Ronnie had been violent towards Betty Lou, although she accused him of violence at later dates, but her habits had been firmly cemented and she continued to display abusive behaviour towards him. She also continued to work at the topless bar, resulting in arrests and thirty days in country jail under the charge of public lewdness. Despite their seven year courtship, the marriage lasted just a year, culminating in Betty Lou Beets's attempted homicide of Ronnie in 1978, where she shot him in the stomach, wounding him, and their divorce in 1979.

She married Doyle Wayne Barker at the age of forty one, closely after her divorce from Threlkold. Their marriage lasted a mere seven weeks before her violent behaviour drove Doyle away from her. However his own violence was undeniable. He had stalked her, assaulted her and raped her during their short relationship. The day he left Betty Lou had bruises all over her face, neck, arms and chest. There is no available record of the divorce, however all living parties assumed it had taken place. However Doyle Wayne did not get out of their marriage unscathed. He disappeared after their divorce and his body was found years later, buried under a garage, killed by three gunshots.

But this grisly deed was not uncovered for many more years to come. Rather, Betty Lou went on to marry a firefighter named Jimmy Don Beets, her final husband, at the age of forty four.

"Jimmy Don Beets was a wonderful man," said a family friend. "He was loved by so many people. An old country boy that a lot people had respect for."

Their courtship would last a mere six months. Betty Lou would meet Jimmy while she worked as a waitress and the seduction began. Her two sons moved in with them. This would be her final marriage, and her actions within it would be her undoing. Although their courtship had been pleasant, they both suffered from alcoholism, which slowly drove their marriage to the same violence she had experienced previously. Less than a year later she murdered him by gunshot, and this time she was caught. Robert Branson, her son from her first marriage, had been informed that she intended to kill her last husband, telling him to steer clear of the residence as the murder took place. On the 6th of August 1983, Robert Branson Junior left their home and Betty Lou Beets committed the gruesome act. Not only did Robert provide evidence that the act was premeditated, but he also was expected to participate. Two hours after leaving the house, Robert Branson Junior returned, finding his step father dead with two gunshot wounds in his body. Rather than seek assistance, Robert Branson Junior, either tainted by a lifetime with a mother who viewed abuse and murder as daily events or himself an individual with low empathy, helped his mother to dispose of the body. Betty Lou Beets and Robert Branson Junior carted Jimmy Don Beets' body outside to an ornamental wishing well that stood in the front yard of their house. Undetected, they cast the body inside.

Then, Betty Lou returned to the house to cover up her acts. She called the police to report her husband missing from their Cedar Creek Lake home. The next day, Betty Lou became more devious. Perhaps inspired, perhaps unnerved by her success killing Doyle Wayne Barker, she realized she needed to create a story with which to divert the police from her trail. Robert Branson Junior recalled to the press how she had taken some of Jimmy Don Beets's heart medication down to his boat at the lake. Then she had removed the propeller, placed the medication in the boat and abandoned it, floating loosely in the water. Later that day, as the twenty four hours since Jimmy Don Beets's initial disappearance drew to a close, various officials began the search for the presumably missing man. Officers from the Henderson County Sheriff's department, various members of the fire department, as well as agents from the Texas Parks and Wildlife department searched for three weeks. They naturally found no body. However they did find Jimmy Don Beets's boat drifting in the lake, near to the Redwood

Beach Marina. There they found his fishing license, an unused life jacket and the heart medication which Betty Lou Beets had placed there. Not knowing anything about the murder or the forged evidence, they brought Betty Lou Beets to the Marina as the sole witness, where she identified the boat and its contents as those of her husband. Although no body had been recovered, it was considered case closed.

Betty Lou Beets would have likely got away with both murders, were it not for confidential information given to the Henderson County Sheriff's Department two years later. The information suggested that Jimmy Don Beets had not disappeared innocently, and that his assumed death, with no body that had been found, may be the result of foul play. The evidence was enough that the cold case was reopened in Spring 1985. As their suspicions became stronger, the investigators were drawn to Betty Lou Beets, who was arrested on the 8th of June of 1985 and then booked into the Henderson County Jail. An officer on the case, Rick Rose, who had been in charge of her arrest warrant, secured a further warrant to search the Beets's home and lands, including the yard. Ultimately, they discovered Jimmy Don Beets's remains buried under the wishing well where he had been left two years prior. But another discovery would surface that would further disturb the case. Also in the back yard was a storage shed which could be moved. When the officers moved it, something compelled them to disturb the soil that had lain there several years. Perhaps it was some confidential evidence or perhaps it was just intuition, but it paid off when they discovered a second body. Doyle Wayne Barker, still missing, was buried there, with three bullets in his body. All five bullets matched the .38 caliber pistol which had been seized from their home after another incident of Betty Lou's violent outbursts. Thanks to the calls she had made the very day of his disappearance there was no room to argue that she had been abusing drugs or alcohol at the time, but there had been no physical evidence that suggested to detectives at the time that Jimmy Don had been abusing her when the incident took place. Her position was weak.

Faced with the evidence, Robert Branson Junior and his sister Shirley finally confessed to their awareness of the killings, as well as their hand in the crimes that had taken place. Not only had Betty Lou told her son about the murder, but she had also informed her daughter, by the Shirley Stegner and not living at the family home, that she planned on killing her husband. Shirley was motivated by her confession to also confess to her involvement in another crime. She told the detectives that she had been involved in the burial of Doyle Wayne Barker's body in October of 1981 after Betty Lou had shot him to death.

In an effort to make herself more likeable to the jury, Betty Lou Beets raised her history of domestic violence as an excuse for her violent behaviour, levying charges against all her prior husbands, as well as her father. However, this would be the first that anyone had heard of most of these charges. This may have been due to attitudes of the times, a desire to protect her children, or the apparently two-sided nature of most of these incidents, however the jury would not believe her claims. They were just too convenient. Instead, it was clear to them that Betty Lou Beets was an unstable and dangerous woman and the only connection between the five men she married and their violence. Whatever the situation was, her psychological well being was never considered during the trial. Despite the obvious impact her upbringing and life would have on her mental state and the fact that her actions up until that point were indicative of definite mental illness, the trial system of the time did not account for that.

Furthermore, the premeditated nature of her actions was evident through her children's abundant testimonials, where they confessed she had shared her intent to kill not only the husbands she managed to murder, but that she had expressed a desire to kill all the men she had been married to. Not only that, but her success concealing the bodies, under the wishing well and under the garden shed, showed a lack of remorse and serious consideration of her crimes. However it seems Betty Lou had not been as careful as she thought. As soon as the trial began, various other witnesses emerged to testify against her. Various people recalled her attempting to collect life insurance of over a hundred thousand dollars as well as a pension of over a thousand dollars a month after Jimmy Don's declared death. A year after the official death of Jimmy Don Beets, she successfully sold his boat, the primary evidence that he had disappeared. She claimed she did not know about his pension or insurance, however seeing as Jimmy Don Beets was already retired and claiming his pension, this claim fell short. Furthermore, had she no awareness of them she would not have pursued either so actively. She claimed she had been told about them when she visited an attorney by the name or E. Ray Andrews about a fire insurance claim she needed to make, at which point he discovered she could claim his insurance and pension. However her own filing for these benefits did not align with the supposed visit, and the only person who could say for sure that she had not known about her deceased husband's finances was E. Ray Andrews himself, who agreed to represent her in exchange for the rights to book and movie deals concerning her life and case.

Betty Lou Beets was indicted for murder for remuneration or the promise of remuneration, with her recovery of his life insurance and pension as evidence. She plead not guilty and was taken to trial, where she was found guilty of the capital offence of first degree murder on the 11th of October of 1985. She was found again guilty during a hearing on the 14th of October 1985 and was sentenced to death by the trial court. This was due to her prior history of violence and attempted murders, which suggested that she would present a threat to others in the future, specifically to any man who entered a relationship with her again. Yet her conviction and sentence were quickly and successfully appealed to the Texas Court of Criminal Appeals. Such was the situation that, under Texas law, crime for the sake of insurance and pension claims was not covered by the definition of "murder for remuneration", instead falling into two separate categories of first degree murder and insurance fraud, or crime with intent to commit insurance fraud. The Texas Court of Criminal Appeals reversed her conviction for capital murder, citing the Texas Penal Code as evidence that her particular case could not be filed as "murder for remuneration". The State then requested a rehearing of the cause. Although her original conviction had been overturned, the fact remained that Betty Lou Beets was guilty of homicide under some circumstance or another.

On the 21st of September of 1988, the Court of Criminal Appeals reinstated her conviction and sentence based on the evidence received. Betty Lou Beets was on death row. Her execution was scheduled for the 8th of November 1989.

However her court case did not go as it should have in the first place. Attorney E. Ray Andrews was heavily invested in sensationalizing her case as much as he could, seeing as he would profit enormously from the case blowing up into a media phenomenon. So although she claimed and he later agreed that she had known nothing of her husband's finances, the trial was conducted under the assumption that she was fully aware of the money she would receive. Not only that, but E. Ray Andrews did everything in his power to create a more dramatic case on both sides, which ultimately meant excluding Betty Lou from much of the information about her own trial. Betty Lou was becoming desperate at this point. Although she had a long history of domestic violence, attempted murder and two bodies in her garden, she decided to attempt to blame the murder of Jimmy Don Beets on Robert Branson Junior, her own son. She did not seem to have made the statement in sound mind, but E. Ray Andrews allowed her to speak on her own behalf and did not retract it, as it added dramatic quality to the event. He tried to cover up later, saying that Betty Lou had possibly been taking the blame for her son, however he had no proof other than that Robert Branson Junior was male and from a rough background. This statement and its acceptance horrified the court, as it was alarming to them to see a mother who, rather than protect her children, was willing to throw them under the bus by falsely accusing them of a crime she had more than evidently committed. Furthermore, by admitting and adhering to the story that Robert Branson Junior was in fact the actual killer, Betty Lou lost all chances of arguing that she acted in self-defence and made her own accusations of domestic violence against Jimmy Don and her prior husbands completely irrelevant. This is despite the fact that a leading domestic violence specialist of the time believed Betty Lou Beets had been significantly mentally impacted by her experiences, and that she suffered "the emotional, cognitive, and behavioural components of battered woman syndrome, rape trauma syndrome, and PTSD" which he added must have interacted with her pre-existing organic brain damage from her childhood illness, history of battering and substance abuse. All together, this would have presented a robust case for her mental illness and need for treatment rather than punishment. However E. Ray Andrews discarded this option in favour of the more dramatic choice of supporting Betty Lou's accusation against her son. They became stuck in the position of having to argue she did not kill her husband at all. This context may have reduced her sentence, or made her eligible to claim insanity. However neither of these options were available.

Throughout the entire case, E. Ray Andrews failed to represent her seriously and did nothing to prevent her from shooting herself in the foot repeatedly. In fact, seeing the case was a lost cause and that he stood to gain more from her sentence than her freedom, Andrews began drinking heavily for the duration of the trial. He chose not to bear witness to her claims that she did not know about Jimmy Don Beets's pension or insurance, which would have transformed the case to one of murder in the context of domestic violence, rather than murder for remuneration. He managed to offer the jury no reasons to consider that Betty Lou was not a serious threat to those around her, eventually sealing her fate. Yet he remained her attorney for the duration of her appeal as well. It was he who raised the point that her financial gain was not necessarily the motivator for murder, but a by product. He also finally raised that she was not aware of the insurance or pension until she spoke to him, however this was met with scepticism due to his negligence to mention it any sooner, and was perceived as a lie in effort to overturn Betty Lou's criminal charges after his initial failure to protect her.

On the 16th of October 1989, Betty Lou filed a motion called a stay of execution which would delay her execution to give her time to prepare and file a habeas corpus application with the state. On the 1st of November she filed the application and the trial court delayed her execution so that the claims she was raising, such as consideration towards her mental state and marital conditions, could be properly addressed. During this time Betty Lou wrote several letters from prison in which she attempted to defend her good name and that of her last husband. She attempted to balance the accusations that she was a black widow by reminding the court that she was Jimmy Don's fourth wife as well. However his previous wives did not come forward to support her. She also defended her own identity, denying that she ever worked as a barmaid, regardless of her own charges for lewd behaviour, and that she was never on welfare, despite her claims after her first divorce. She also said that the Fire Department Chaplain, who stated he had informed her about Beets's insurance and pension, had spoken to her sister in law, Betty Beets, instead. She even quibbled over the descriptions of her garden, insisting the well was a planter in the shape of a well and not an actual well. It was clear that Betty Lou Beets was desperate to save face and project a more pleasant, more ordinary identity than the one which E. Ray Andrews had created for her in the courtroom. It was also clear that her mental health was degrading as she endured life in prison and submitted her habeas corpus petition. In her petition she argued against her sentence of the death penalty, raising issues such as the alleged value Jimmy Don Beets apparently added the community, the testimonials of victims and sufferers whose statements were unconstitutional under the Victim Impact Statements act of 1987, and the poor assistance which E. Ray Andrews provided, especially regarding her history of domestic abuse. Yet without his help in writing and presenting the letter, her claims were weak and not fully backed by legal evidence. Andrews did not visit her from the point of her sentencing and prepared for her trials without ever speaking to her. Furthermore, she could have claimed that his services were provided against American Bar Association rules, which prohibit the trade of legal services for copyright issues, such as the rights to her case. None of this was raised by her against him, and as such it was not considered during her habeas corpus appeal.

However on the 27th of June her appeal for state habeas corpus was turned away. She was placed in the position of proving that, had E. Ray Andrews presented a testimony about her lack of awareness of the insurance and her history of domestic violence, the jury would have judged her not guilty of a capital crime. Without a proper attorney to defend her, it would be impossible for Betty Lou to prove this was the case, and the court deemed Andrews's mistakes to have been harmless to her trial. The Fifth Circuit Court of Appeals went on to turn down her final appeals. The judges remained convinced that, regardless of any remaining evidence, Betty Lou Beets's history of violence and attempted murder, along with the two concealed bodies in her garden, were evidence enough that a death sentence was a fair response to the crime that had taken place. She had displayed violence her whole life, even towards men who had not presented a threat to her, and had attempted to kill all but one of her husbands. She had concealed her murders carefully and for many years and was willing to place the blame on her own adult son. In other words, regardless of her own situation, her criminal intent was viewed as evident and incorrigible, and her death sentence was the only fitting end to her crime spree.

On death row, Betty Lou Beets retained some supporters, mostly her own children. Some of Betty Lou's daughters went to E. Ray Andrews with photographic evidence of the domestic abuse she had suffered in order to request a parole review, but were declined. They insisted on presenting the evidence that she had suffered and that her acts of violence were a result of brain damage and abuse, not of malicious intent. Faye Lane, one of her daughters, insisted that her mother would only have done anything so horrific if she believed she was abused. Domestic violence awareness groups and charities acting against the death sentence appealed to have her sentence changed to a life sentence in prison, based not only on her own suffering, but on their universal stance against the irreversible process of the death penalty. Yet even those defending her maintained that she was a violent, unpredictable woman and not safe to exit into the general public.

And not all her children were so kind. Shirley told the press that Doyle Wayne Barker was killed because he owned the trailer where they lived, and that after the divorce which Barker had initiated, Betty Lou and her children would be evicted from the trailer and left homeless. This set a precedent where even her own daughter could not believe that Betty Lou was completely unaware of the financial benefits of murdering Jimmy Don Beets, especially not after she had successfully killed Barker. Knowing that she was still doubted and seeing hope as ever distant, Betty Lou composed her memoirs from death row, presenting her case.

Beets turned to her last resort which was to appeal to then-governor George W. Bush to spare her life. After a media incident where he jokingly insulted the last woman to be executed in Texas in an insensitive manner, George W. Bush seemed keen to prove he had no bias against women, even in the prison system, and agreed to review her case. This would have meant hearing the witnesses which had not been heard by the trial lawyer and present a case against her execution based on the circumstances of her life, including medical and psychiatric evidence. He could have granted her a thirty day reprieve in which he made his decision, however this never materialized. His number was made available and he received thousands of calls and letters from people urging him to spare her, with only fifty seven endorsing her sentence. Yet he did not grant the reprieve or halt the execution.

Betty Lou Beets was finally executed on the 24th of February of 2000, via lethal injection. Protestors from various organisations gathered outside as her sentence awaited. She declined both her last meal and her final statement, having been given by then enough time to make sense of what was happening and to say everything which needed to be said. Strapped to the death chamber gurney, she received her injection at six pm and died within eighteen minutes. She was sixty two years old. She left behind five adult children, nine grandchildren and six great-grandchildren, as well as her memoirs. Her story may be shocking, and it may be hard to pick sides at times, but that is exactly why her trial presents a solid case against the black and white ideals the court system held regarding crime and punishment, perpetrator and victim, defence and offence. Someone can at once be a victim of horrific crimes and a perpetrator of them, at once be a defendant and raise accusations, at once deserve punishment yet suffer a crime gone unpunished. There is no doubt that Betty Lou Beets was a violent woman who invited violence into her own life, an alcoholic and a murderer. However there is no doubt either that she was a good mother within her capacity, a victim of a series of horrific crimes, a disabled person with a background she could not escape and a desperate woman who saw no way out of her situation. Neither black nor white, good not bad, Betty Lou Beets sits in the grey areas of the law.

THE REAL GONE GIRL : THE TRUE STORY OF MICHELLE THEER

29

DARLA PUGH

At first glance, Michelle Theer looked like the stereotypical bored housewife. She married an Air Force captain who was deployed on assignment for long periods of time. Her days were spent alone and idle.

And you know what they say about idle hands.

Michelle felt unfulfilled in her marriage and didn't so much want out, she wanted something more. Attractive with long brown hair and arched eyebrows, Michelle did not have any problems attracting members of the opposite sex. She needed something discreet, however, something that would simply titillate her fantasies and relief the boredom that she would suffer during the long absences of her husband.

So she turned to the Internet.

It started innocently at first. A few keystrokes of flirtatious messages. Some a bit racier than others, but where was the harm? She was hiding behind a computer monitor. It isn't cheating if there is no face to face, Michelle thought.

Then she came across the profile of John Diamond. His pictures showed him to be a tall and muscular man, a special forces soldier that made Michelle's heart skip a beat.

Or maybe she saw him as the perfect foil. The perfect fall guy to get rid of her husband.

Their flirtations started innocently enough. Then the messages got racier and racier until they both felt the need to satiate their fantasies for one another.

Those fantasies led to sex.

Then murder.

Frank Theer, better known as "Marty", was a quiet and reserved young man. In high school, his friends introduced him to what they believed what be his perfect match.

Michelle Forcier.

Michelle was outgoing, bubbly and only sixteen when she met Marty who was a year older. Her friends believed that Michelle's extroverted personality could be a counterweight to Marty's introverted nature. Marty had originally intended to become an astronaut, his ambition and intelligence made him an attractive catch to Michelle. They were both the product of military families, both moving a lot as children so they had a kinship there. Both were ambitious and had concrete plans for the future. Marty would join the Air Force. Michelle would join the reserves and serve in the Gulf War.

"Michelle had ambition," forensic psychologist Paula Orange said. "She wanted status and respect. But she grew up in a military family and succumbed to the tribalism and social pressures that existed in that kind of environment. You grow up, get married and have kids. Michelle probably had mixed feelings about that. She wanted to do her own thing. So, in essence, she was living a double life from the get-go. She was doing the expected thing of getting married but on the side she was the libertine, drinking heavily and having extra-marital affairs."

The couple would maintain their long-distance relationship for four years until Michelle was assigned to the

Persian Gulf War in 1991. Thinking that their courtship had lasted long enough, Marty asked Michelle to marry him.

Michelle, at twenty years old, said yes to the other man she had known up until that point.

Their wedding video would show the couple to be a happy one. They kissed for the cameras and fed each other wedding cake.

"We did everything together," Michelle said. "He treated me really well. I just thought we had the perfect relationship. We were best friends."

The couple would remain married for six years as Marty's Air Force assignments forced them to move from base to base. Michelle had fantasized about going to exotic locations overseas. Instead, Marty's tenure was limited to uninspiring outposts in Oklahoma, Alabama and Florida.

Places that would bore Michelle to tears.

"Michelle was getting lonely," Orange said. "Like so many military families, these things take shape early on. Marty would be gone months at a time and of course telephone and e-mail exchanges are not the same as a face to face. Michelle felt entitled to more from life then what she was getting. This isn't uncommon obviously but Michelle took things one step further eventually."

During the occasions when Marty was on leave, he and Michelle would often end up fighting.

"I want children," Marty said.

"No way," Michelle would shake her head, stifling a laugh.

"Then what's the point? What's the point of being married if we are not going to start a family?"

"Raise children in this shithole? You've got to be kidding."

The arguments would escalate. Michelle was a slob, refusing to clean up around the house. Marty would complain but Michelle would deflect and criticize him for his poor career choice.

"You're never home," Michelle hissed. "And you want a family?"

After nine years of marriage, Marty was sent to the Pope Air Force Base near Fayetteville, North Carolina. Fayetteville was considered to be the equivalent of Siberia when it came to transfers. Military members gave the town nicknames like FayetteNam, Fatalville, and FayetteHell. Michelle found the town to be even worse than its reputation when it came to providing excitement.

"Here I was in Fayetteville," Michelle said. "'Loserville'. And I had nobody I could hang out with. Nobody I could pick up a phone and call."

Marty saw things differently, writing on a Christmas card in 2000, "Pope has provided a great change of pace for me and Michelle is happy with her new job. So, 2000 is looking good for both of us."

Michelle would suffer from depression and loneliness after the six years of marriage. Marty tried hard to appease his high-maintenance wife. He took her scuba diving in the

Caribbean, skiing in the Rockies, parachuting in Georgia and then a summer marathon run in Alaska.

Despite all of the adventures, Michelle was dissatisfied. She wanted something more out of life, more excitement. She decided to go back to school and earn a degree in psychology. She felt desperately alone, however, as Marty would once again be deployed overseas. Michelle would find work with a psychologist named Dr. Thomas Harbin's and work to obtain her license in psychology.

Still, it wasn't enough. She needed excitement.

More specifically, sexual excitement.

So she turned to the Internet.

Michelle began turning to dating sites. She noodled around with different memberships and it never became more than an idle pursuit to fill the hours of loneliness. Setting up her ad with the headline of "sexy brunette seeks rendezvous man", her inbox was immediately deluged with drooling suitors.

She entertained a number of different men, sending and receiving flirty messages. Michelle had become interested in the local "swinger" and sex club scene, advertising for a man who would be her escort to a club called "Carolina Friends."

One man got her attention more than the others.

JOHN DIAMOND

John was four years younger than Michelle, entering the United States Army during the year in which the couple got married. He had a wandering eye, currently married to his second wife knew of his lothario ways. She was a Panamanian woman who was a few years older than John. He didn't hide his infidelities and on one occasion had one of his girlfriends call the house to ask his wife if John was still meeting her at the beach.

"John loved women," Debbie Dvorak, John's younger sister said. "He loved women, he always had a girlfriend and was a ladies man. My brother was an attractive guy. He had a great personality. His personality made him that much more attractive."

John's background was remarkably similar to Marty in that he was born into a military family. His father was a Vietnam veteran and his grandfather had been a POW during World War II. John himself became an Army ranger and was stationed nearby at Fort Bragg. He was trained as a sniper and highly decorated. Their military backgrounds were where their similarities ended, however. Marty was highly respected as a pilot and a family man. John was a good soldier but nowhere near the honorable family man Marty was.

"John was a highly regarded soldier," Orange said. "But he already had two families. He had a child with his first wife and they divorced. He remarried and had a son with the second wife. So his plate was already full by the time he met Michelle Theer."

John and Michelle both intuitively knew what the other wanted. They both needed the adrenaline, the excitement of forbidden sex to add spice to their humdrum lives. John and Michelle spent months sending each other flirtatious and juicy e-mails before realizing it was time to put fantasy aside and meet for real.

There was an immediate attraction as they met at a Fayetteville coffee shop.

"It was love at first sight," John said.

"I thought he was very, very charming," Michelle said. "He was funny. We talked about movies and music. Things that me and Marty didn't talk about."

They were both still married, however, and that added to the thrill.

LET THE SEDUCTION BEGIN

John and Michelle then began spending as much time with they could with one another. Their extra-marital affair could be done inside Michelle's own bedroom as Marty would be stationed overseas. Michelle grew addicted to the sex, the excitement and the adoration that John gave her.

"He was very attentive," Michelle said. "He was very affectionate. He was very adoring. Yeah, it felt great."

The sex grew addicting for both John and Michelle. Like drug addicts, they found escape through the pleasures of the flesh. E-mails and text messages between the two would reveal a controlling relationship that favored Michelle. He was at her beck and call, like a "puppy dog" said one investigator.

"I can't wait until you come back so we can take care of each other," John wrote in one message. "You know, sex, sex, sex and of course...more sex. I know that we are meant to be together and are kindred soul mates. I will always love you, no matter how you have hurt me."

"I think it was just the sex," Dvorak said when asked what John saw in the married Michelle. "He was obsessed. He was smitten with having sex with her."

Michelle would later reveal to her psychologist that she didn't think that the affair took away from her love for Marty.

"She said that Marty was the love of her life," Orange said. "With John, it was just lust. She never loved him the same way she loved Marty. At least that is how she differentiated and rationalized it in her mind."

Without fear of being caught, the two began going to dance clubs as well as "swinger parties" as a couple at Michelle's request.

"She would take him to these sex clubs," Dvorak said. "She would say 'If you want to go have sex with her, that's okay. That's fine. Go. I'm fine with it.' And he was just like 'Wow, okay.'"

Finding a partner in crime for her sex addiction, Michelle indulged whenever she could.

Then Marty returned home.

REPAIR JOB?

Marty had been undergoing flight maneuvers in Little Rock, Arkansas. When he returned home to Fayetteville, he came back knowing that his marriage was on the rocks. Michelle wanted to go to marriage counseling but Marty refused.

"He wouldn't agree to marriage counseling and I moved out," Michelle said. "He was shocked."

Michelle got her own place that summer. She would spend most of her days and nights in the arms of John Diamond. "He was so attentive," Michelle recalled. "He would rub my feet for five hours if I wanted him to."

John continued to fall deeper in love with Michelle. He thought that she was more intelligent than the women he had dated before, more of a challenge. Three months after living alone, however, Michelle changed her mind about John.

She went back to Marty.

Michelle thought she would give the marriage one more chance. Marty relented on going to counseling and the couple hashed things out with the therapist.

"I want Michelle to clean up around the house more," Marty said to the counselor. "I mean, I know that with women's lib and all that sounds very degrading. But I work my tail off. I'm away for months at a time and would at least like to come home to someplace clean. It shows respect. Coming home to a mess of a house shows a lot of disrespect."

"See what I mean?" Michelle said. "Talk about obsessive-compulsive. Where does a clean house fit in the grand scheme of things? I want to live life. Go out and have new experiences. But this guy? All he wants to do is stay home. Stay home in his clean house."

The counseling didn't work. In the summer of 2000, Michelle moved out of the family home. She and John found an off-base apartment and began living together. The cheating couple took a vacation to the Netherlands Antilles and fell in love with the place. Michelle enjoyed it so much that she applied to the Saba School of Medicine. She listed John as her next of kin, describing his relationship to her as "fiancee".

But later Michelle would tell her psychologist that her decision to go back with John was a "relapse."

"I knew that I loved Marty," Michelle said. "And I knew that I wanted to make it work. I knew it in my heart."

Then she went back to Marty again.

She continued to see John, however, but the relationship would be on and off. John would plead his case through e-mails, writing flowery messages about how much he loved Michelle.

"I love you so much," John wrote. "I know you feel the same. What I don't understand is how you could be with a man that you don't love anymore. You're unhappy with him. You're happy with me. This is all so confusing."

"He said specifically 'I'm going to kill myself,' Michelle said. "'I can't live without you. You can't do this to me. I'm gonna go drive my car off a bridge.'"

According to Michelle, John would not relent in his pursuit of her. He would show up at her office and make a scene, telling her that he would tell Marty about their affair.

Michelle relented to seeing John one last time, agreeing to meet with John at a local restaurant. According to her statements to her psychologist, she went there in the hopes of ending the affair for good.

"We had that whole talk," Michelle said. "You know, 'we can only be friends' and 'this can never happen again. Never, never, never.' He seemed very calm. Very rational. I told him, 'I don't want to leave my husband.' I never told him, 'I love you.' I never said 'I want to be with you.' I mean, I think I was pretty straight up."

Whether this conversation took place or not, it certainly landed on deaf ears to John. He continued to pursue Michelle and they continued to see one another.

"She probably led him on a roller coaster ride of emotions," military investigator Vincent Bustillo said. "Brought him to the peak, thinking everything was going to be good and they're going to leave this life together, off in some Caribbean island, and then back off and leave Diamond emotionally distraught to the point where that's what he wanted and nothing was going to get in his way."

The on-again, off-again relationship turned red hot by December 9th, 2000. Michelle told Marty that she would be attending a birthday party for a graduate school friend of hers. Thinking nothing of it, Marty simply nodded his head.

Michelle left the home and met John for a night of torrid sex.

"The manipulation began early on in the relationship," Orange said. "Michelle would pull John into her world with sex. Then she would push him away by going back to her husband. John was smitten with her and could not let go.

He would have done anything for her and Michelle knew it. An Army ranger willing to do anything for you is a powerful thing. It was like having her own personal soldier willing to kill. But who did she need getting rid of and why?"

Michelle knew that Marty had a half-million dollar insurance policy that he took out in 1999.

She was the sole beneficiary.

John's sister, however, remained adamant that Michelle had written those lovelorn letters to herself in order to put the trail on John Diamond.

"He never once expressed any feelings of love for her to me," Debbie Dvorak said. "Unless you come to me with a handwritten letter that he was obsessed with her, I'll never believe that. He told me he did not want to marry her. He did not want to spend the rest of his life with her. I think she was obsessed with him. Obsessed that she couldn't control him. That she couldn't control the situation."

Eight days later after her latest rendezvous, Michelle would attend a Christmas party given by her employer, Dr. Thomas Harbin. She brought along Marty who seemed to enjoy the company at the otherwise mellow party. About an hour into the get-together, Michelle excused herself to make a phone call.

A phone call to John Diamond.

A short while later, Marty and Michelle drove another couple home before heading to the local gas station.

"We ended up turning around and going back to the office," Michelle said. "To get some stuff that I needed so I could stay up and work that night."

Marty sat in their Ford Explorer and watched as Michelle walked up to the second story office. A few minutes passed and Marty got worried. He got out of the car and went upstairs to her office to make sure his wife was okay.

He reached the top of the stairs and then he was ambushed.

A gunman stepped out from the shadows and fired four times. Marty tumbled down the stairwell. When he reached the bottom, he was still alive.

The shadowy gunman stood above him and fired one more time, killing Marty.

Michelle would state to police that she discovered Marty's body and began screaming his name. She said that she thought he was still breathing but in the haste of living her office she locked her keys inside. Michelle said she ran two miles to a video store to call 911 despite the area having numerous homes and businesses nearby.

Police arrived on scene and found Michelle cradling Marty in her arms, her husband's blood pooling onto the concrete. Military police arrived shortly after the city authorities, getting the case after it was revealed that Marty was an Air Force Captain.

Both police agencies initially suspected that Marty was the victim of a random robbery. They searched the area and found no one despite the fact that Michelle stated that she has "seen someone in the bushes" when she discovered Marty's body.

FIGURING THINGS OUT

Investigators would discover bullet holes at the top of the stairwell as well as sequins from Marty's suit. They surmised that Marty was at the top of the stairwell when he was shot from someone coming from the bottom of the steps. He then fell down the stairs, bleeding but still alive when the attacker delivered the fatal shot to the back of his left ear.

The police then found his wallet with cash and credit cards still on his person. The scene now looked less like a robbery and more like a targeted execution. After recovering the shell casings (a 9mm pistol was the culprit) they went upstairs to Michelle's office. Inside, they discovered that Michelle had used the toilet (and didn't flush) as well as leaving an empty candy wrapper in the trash.

Police noted that it was almost as if she went upstairs to wait *something* out. If she were, in fact, looking for a book, it would not have taken that long.

The police released Michelle on her own recognizance. The next morning, they returned to the office and spoke to her employer, Dr. Harbin. The doctor would reveal that Michelle had been having marital trouble and was having an affair with John Diamond.

Police now saw John Diamond as the man with the motive. But when they interviewed Lourdes Diamond, John's wife, she said that she was home with her husband that entire evening, watching a movie. The police became discouraged.

Then Lourdes added that John got a call about 9 p.m. that evening and that he quickly left the house. She stated that John changed his clothes, put on parka clothing and told her that he had to go to the barracks.

Police then checked out the phone records on John's cell phone and noted that he did receive a call from Michelle.

Michelle would later deny that she ever called John that night.

After receiving the cell phone records, however, it became evident that John and Michelle had called each other twenty times a day at a minimum. They had exchanged a phone call about ninety minutes prior to Marty being shot to death.

When pressed on his involvement with Michelle, John admitted to the affair.

"She is one of many," John said. "She's a side piece. I have a lot of women."

Michelle would later claim that she conducted her own detective work after Marty's death. She stated that she went to John's home and asked him if he knew anything about the murder.

"I asked him 'do you know anything about this," Michelle said. "'Do you know anybody who had anything to do with this?' He said 'No, I would never do anything to hurt you. I know how much you loved him.' I believed him. He looked so trustful."

Police would dismiss Michelle's confrontation with John. They tailed him around town, watching him park in front of the Theer home and sneak inside through the back door.

John would remain there the whole night.

"He knew I was depressed," Michelle said. "And I was getting more and more depressed. I think I went to John for comfort."

John and Michelle would then travel to Florida as Marty's murder investigation was ongoing. The official reason according to Michelle:

Grief counseling.

She claimed there was a former professor there in the state that would be able to help her cope with Marty's death.

While in Florida, John went to live with his sister, Debbie Dvorak.

"He acted as if nothing was wrong," Dvorak said. "He knows he had nothing to do with it. He didn't shoot him."

The physical evidence remained weak. The police continued to sift through the cell phone records and came across the phone number of one of John's army friends. Calling him up, they asked if John would have access to any 9mm weaponry. The friend would reveal that he had, in fact, loaned out his gun to John. The transaction took place just days before Marty's murder. The Smith & Wesson Model 5906 that he loaned John would be the same type of weapon used to kill Marty. All the police had to do was obtain the murder weapon and they would have the physical evidence required to indict.

Then, as if on cue in a mystery movie, John Diamond reported a break-in of his car in the base parking lot.

"Did they steal anything?" a reporting officer asked.

"Yeah," John said. "My friend's gun. Jesus, he's going to be pissed."

But John made a mistake.

There was a pile of glass outside the car which would indicate that the passenger side door had been open during the "break-in". John had smashed the window himself and feared getting glass on the interior of his car.

The US Army investigators would charge John with obstruction of justice, conspiracy, and premeditated murder. The Army officials relayed their findings to civilian police and wanted them to charge Michelle. Five months later, John would be court-martialed. Michelle would be called as a witness but invoke her Fifth Amendment right with every question.

"John would have a cocky air about him throughout his trial," Orange said. "He joked with reporters and smiled at the jury. He felt certain that he would be acquitted."

His cocky demeanor would backfire. The jury would find John guilty and he was convicted of all counts. His current wife Lourdes would testify that John would receive a phone call in the evening and leave the home. His mother-in-law would also testify that he had come home in the middle of the night and began washing clothes.

John would be sentenced to life without parole.

But Michelle Theer remained free.

"What I got from him (John) after he was arrested was that he didn't want anything to do with her," his sister Debbie said. "Nothing. You don't expect to be convicted on theory. On myths. Show me blood. Show me a gun. Show me a time-line that works. Show me those facts. I'll believe until the day I die that she (Michelle) killed her husband, that she planned to have my brother go down for it, so she could live this happy, wonderful life."

"From my opinion, if he (John) wanted to shoot someone he could have shot someone from a mile away. Why sneak up on somebody and shoot them five times and even according to the coroner, they're all over the place. Whoever shot that weapon wasn't a sharp shooter. Didn't know how to shoot a weapon, was scared to be there, whatever, they were all over the place. Ricocheting off of this and ricocheting off of that. There's just no way."

Upon John's conviction, Michelle left town. She moved to New Orleans until the Fayetteville police finally got the grand jury to indict her on charges of first-degree murder in May of 2002.

Michelle fled the city, however, and became a fugitive on the run.

"I think she planned to kill her husband a long time ago," Dvorak said. "I think she waited and researched and waited for that right person who would look and fit the part to pin it on."

During John's trial, Michelle had begun her preparation. She purchased pamphlets such as REBORN IN THE USA, HOW TO DISAPPEAR IN AMERICA, and SECRETS FOR GETTING A NEW IDENTITY, obtaining tips on how to evade detection from authorities. Michelle also obtained a few books on learning Spanish and travel guides to several Latin countries like Mexico. She bleached her hair blonde and used a high-end printer to make both fake birth and baptismal certificates.

Michelle was dead serious about evading capture. Hiding out in Florida, she paid to have plastic surgery done on her nose, chin and had laser surgery to remove her acne and other skin blemishes.

From an appearance standpoint, she had fully reinvented herself. Michelle was able to fool the DMV and get a driver's license under the alias of "Alexandra Solomon." She rented an apartment under the name of "Lisa Pendragon" from Cynthia Geesey in Lauderdale by the Sea, Florida.

"She told me that she was on the run from an abusive boyfriend in California," Geesey said. "I thought she was well-spoken and articulate."

Geesey allowed Michelle to sign the six-month lease, believing her story. Michelle would blend into her surroundings rather easily. She made a few friends around the neighborhood and found a new boyfriend. She then called her parents from a pay phone in town to let them know she was okay.

"She was always a little apprehensive," Geesey said. "Always looking over her shoulder. That's the only thing I found a little strange about her. I was talking to her one day in front of her apartment and there was a helicopter overhead. And she freaked out! Ran back inside. I said 'It's just a helicopter' and she said 'I don't know, it might be my boyfriend.' And I found that a little odd. But other than that she seemed pretty reasonable , paid her rent on time. Took good care of her animals, no other problems with her."

Fayetteville police were at a loss in locating Michelle and enlisted the aid of United States Marshals. True to form, they knew that Michelle could not resist male companionship and caught a break. Michelle instructed her new boyfriend to call her parents from a pay phone in order to relay a message. Her new beau, however, made the mistake of calling Michelle's family from his parent's home. The U.S. Marshals were already tracing all of Michelle's calls and they quickly found out the identity of her new boyfriend.

Placing him under watch, Michelle's new beau soon led authorities straight to her.

After being on the run for three months, Michelle had been finally been captured.

THE AFTERMATH

Michelle's case took two years to go to trial. She would turn down a plea deal which would send her to prison for only ten years. The case then went to trial for ten weeks, drawing both local and national media attention.

Despite the lengthy trial, the jury returned after only six hours of deliberation.

Marty Theer's mother, Linda, waited in nervous anticipation as the verdict was read.

"Guilty."

Linda shook with emotion and tears as the word was spoken. For her, she felt relief that the trial was finally over.

"He (Marty) was a very, very tender person," Linda said. "There wasn't a mean bone in his body. He wouldn't have anything bad to say about anybody. I wish I could say the same."

Michelle would be sentenced to life in prison without the possibility of parole. She is currently housed at the North Carolina Correctional Institute for Women in Raleigh, North Carolina.

John is currently imprisoned at the United States Disciplinary Barracks at Fort Leavenworth, Kansas.

Both John and Michelle have made attempts to obtain a new trial without success.

THE BONDAGE MURDERS : THE TRUE STORY OF SHIRLEY WITHERS

MARY MAXWELL

Shirley Withers and Peter Shellard looked to be a mismatched couple.

Shellard was a multi-millionaire dollar real estate mogul and high-end car dealer. Logic would dictate that he would date much younger women, seducing aspiring actresses and models with his wealth. But Shirley was anything but a supermodel. She was an ordinary looking bookkeeper, thirty-three-years-old, and bit on the frumpy side.

"He was a hot shot," forensic psychologist Paula Orange said. "An eccentric hotshot but still very well-to-do. He would strut around town wearing fancy suits with matching socks but wear sandals over them. Shirley, on the other hand, was very unassuming. She looked like the typical cubicle drone. A little overweight and plain looking. Nothing sexy about her."

Their relationship, however, would be one of the biggest firestorms of sex, murder, and drugs in Australian history.

BEGINNINGS

Shirley was born in New Delhi, India in 1966. She immigrated with her family to Australia when she was a child. She married young and had two sons with her first husband. By 2000, she would be divorced and immediately be on the market for a new beau.

Enter Peter Shellard.

Peter, born in 1949, touted himself as a self-made millionaire although he had a benefactor in an older, maternal figure in Vera Moore.

He didn't finish high school, dropping out to obtain his real estate agent's license at night. Once he acquired that, he began leveraging properties around the Brighton area eventually making a fortune in addition to buying a high-end car dealership.

He called his company "Peter Shellard Real Estate" and then used that money to help finance a deal where he took control over Kellow-Falkiner Motors. He juggled both real estate as well as used Rolls-Royce and Bentley parts.

Shellard's businesses continued to flourish. He purchased many companies as well as commercial and rental properties.

"He hung around some heavy hitters in his area," Orange said. "People who could buy Rolls Royces without batting an eye."

Shellard would purchase the Rosecraddock Place in North Caulfield, a regal mansion which would later sell for over $7 million upon his death. As his wealth grew, he began collecting high-end cars which included a 1923 Rolls-Royce, a 1951 Rolls-Royce Silver Dawn, and a Mercedez-Benz 450SL convertible.

AN ECCENTRIC NUT

Shellard did have mental issues, however, suffering from bipolar disorder.

"His mansion was filled with all kinds of knick-knacks," Orange said. "Stuff that seemed disconnected and junky. But he was bipolar and people with that ailment tend to have different eccentricities. His was to hoard stuff among other things."

Shellard was reported to be a recluse, sheltering himself from the outside world as he became more wealthy. He had a barbed wire fence built high around the mansion but it served more to keep him in then keeping people out. His neighbors would rarely see him outside the compound unless he was walking his dogs. He also had ponies and kept an area for beehives. Neighbors complained about the bees and the city had the hives destroyed. Shellard would later file suit and demand that he have the remains of his dead bees returned.

Shellard would treat other homeowners as if they were peasants and would come and go on their private grounds as he pleased. One neighbor reported that Shellard came into their backyard and began sifting through their garden tools. Another complained that Shellard would park one of his Rolls-Royces in their personal garage. Shellard was informed to remove the vehicle after which he became enraged and began to tear apart the garage. He would then be sued for the action and was forced to pay almost $2000 in damages.

"Obviously, he walked around as if he had a sense of entitlement," Orange said. "Definitely a narcissistic sociopath but he could turn on the charm when he wanted. It all depended on what he wanted. When he was trying to make a sale, he could charm you. When he was doing something stupid and you called him on it, that is when he went berserk."

Town councilwoman Veronika Martens had plenty of bizarre dealings with Shellard as well. On one occasion, Shellard chopped down some cypress trees on his property and began burning the branches. Neighbors called to complain and firefighters came down to extinguish the flames.

Enraged, Shellard began attacking the firefighters and cut through the fire hoses with an ax.

Later, Shellard would be caught breaking into Caulfield Town Hall by climbing in through the roof. He would also come into the building unannounced, enter unoccupied offices and begin making phone calls.

"Shellard was an aggressive, anti-government guy," Orange said. "He went so far as to try to have his mansion designated as a religious place in order to avoid taxes. The judge got a good laugh at that one. The religion of what? Nutty behavior?"

Angered that his request was denied, he began making plans to tear down the mansion and divide up the land. But legal maneuverings blocked him from doing that as city council members had his mansion placed on the Historic Buildings Council, giving it legal protection.

A SADO-MASOCHIST

A ladies man, Shellard would marry twice. He had three daughters, Jenny, Clare and Sarah, before divorcing his second wife Elizabeth in 1994.

Shellard really did not have any bad habits that than his eccentricities as he abstained from both alcohol and smoking. He did have one fetish, however, and that was sadomasochism.

Shellard would go to clubs and participate in bondage sessions, preferring visits to the Hellfire Club in Brighton. Once there, he would "dress up in a full range of leather outfits and had belts with studs."

Shellard would go to the Hellfire Club to be whipped.

"He told me initially that his pain threshold was very low," Shellard's friend Christine Smith said. "And after a number of visits his tolerance for pain increased to the point where he really liked what was occurring. He found it very erotic."

By 2001, he was looking for a new partner and found one in Shirley Withers.

"Initially mum and I thought Shirley was a bit odd," Jenny, Shellard's eldest daughter recalled. "She would never look you in the eye. She was always very kind, though."

ENTER SHIRLEY WITHERS

Opposites attract, and Shellard soon began wooing Shirley with his luxurious lifestyle. He brought her numerous gifts, jewelry, and clothing.

"I'll bankroll all your dreams," he teased.

Shirley took him up on the offer, expressing her desire to run her own clothing boutique.

"Shellard did anything and everything for Shirley," forensic psychologist Paula Orange said. "He bought her everything she asked for evening financing her 'dream' of running a boutique store in a prestigious area of Brighton. Never mind the fact that Shirley had no business experience. Shellard believed he had money to burn."

"You can't be serious?" Shirley gushed when Peter told her he would buy her a clothing company.

"What are you going to call it?" Shellard asked, smiling.

"God," Shirley said. "God. I don't know. How about Suzette? Suzette Boutique?"

"Suzette Boutique!" Shellard laughed aloud as Shirley hugged him in appreciation.

Shellard made all the arrangements for Shirley to run the store. He had it designed and built to her specifications.

Shirley would have all of the brand name fashions in her store. She loaded the shelves with Marianna Hardwick, Charlie Brown, and Lisa Ho.

Shellard had one caveat and that was having his eldest daughter, Jenny, work in the boutique. Jenny herself, however, had a less than flattering impression of both Shirley and her attempts to run a business.

"My first impression when I started working there was that it was just a mess," Jenny said. "I couldn't understand how Shirley kept paying us every week. I had seen invoices totaling thousands of dollars and wondered where Shirley was getting the money. Shirley would just continuously buy stock for the business and for herself. She definitely had a problem with spending money."

Shellard did not stop at just buying Shirley her own boutique.

He bought her a house.

"It was a bit of an odd arrangement," Orange said. "They had separate living quarters. Shellard wanted his own house to himself and would visit Shirley for coital purposes."

Shellard displayed further bad judgment when he allowed Shirley to be put in charge of the accounting of his car dealership.

"He figured she was a bookkeeper," Orange said. "She must know what she's doing."

Shellard's naivete didn't end there as he allowed Shirley access to his property accounts in addition to becoming a signatory on his car dealership.

What Shellard didn't take into account was that Shirley was not a person he could trust nor did she know what she was doing.

Her boutique began to fail. She had purchased too much product and the few items that did sell would not have a high enough margin. Being a marginal business person, she continued to purchase inventory despite not generating any revenue.

The store began losing money. Lost of it.

So Shirley took it upon herself to begin stealing from Shellard's dealership. She would write checks to herself in upwards of $10,000. Shellard began noticing the discrepancies and called in his accountant.

After checking the books, the two realized that Shirley stole over $900,000, a significant amount of Shellard's wealth.

NO CURE FOR A SPENDAHOLIC

Shellard owned over eleven properties and his total net worth looked to be about $10-15 million.

By the time Shellard had finally got wind of Shirley's financial doings, she had amassed over $43,000 in credit card debt while her store was almost $275,000 in the red.

"She simply had no idea what she was doing," Orange said. "She spent and spent and spent."

To top it off, she had siphoned nearly a million dollars from the dealership account, funding the boutique and her own shopping sprees.

"She's robbing you blind," the accountant said. "You should go to the police."

"I'll take care of it," Shellard said. "Let me handle it."

Shellard began to take action. He informed his bank that he wanted Shirley removed as the signatory for his automotive dealership. Then he called a meeting with his friend, Eugene Hand and his lawyer Stuart Winston

"She's ripping me off," Shellard said. "The bitch is robbing me blind. She shuttled over $150,000 into her own account."

"You need to call the police," Winston said.

"I'm going to sell her house," Shellard said. "Fuck her. I need to recoup that loss."

Shellard then confronted Shirley about stealing his money. He was livid, demanding to know what she had been doing.

"He obviously felt betrayed," Orange said. "He was crazier than a shithouse rat, but let's face it, the guy had been good to her. He bought her everything she wanted and let her join him in this decadent lifestyle. But it wasn't good enough for her. She stole his credit cards. Wrote checks in his name payable to her."

Shirley didn't feel remorse at the dressing down by Shellard. She just didn't want the gravy train to leave.

THAT MONEY AIN'T GOING NOWHERE

Shirley began looking for a solution. She noticed a scraggly, down and out woman visiting her boutique often and a light bulb went on her head.

The woman was named Sophia.

Sensing she was a person with some wrong side of the street connections, Shirley saw Sophia and her boyfriend Stanley as "useful idiots" in a plot to kill her husband. They were low-level drug dealers willing to do anything for a buck.

Even if it included murder.

"Shirley gave them a song and dance about how she was an abused spouse," Orange said. "She told the two junkies that she had to endure nightly beatings and rapes. How Shellard would tie her up and have his way with her."

Sophia and Stanley, despite being heroin addicts and petty criminals, felt moral indignation.

Then Shirley waved a few thousand dollars in their face and they were willing to do whatever she asked.

On May 6th, 2005, Shirley lead the two junkies into Shellard's home.

"He's sound asleep in his bed until Shirley attacks him, placing a pillow case over his head," Orange said. "The two junkies hold Shellard down but he begins to fight. He struggles with Sophia and bites her finger. The junkie screams and takes some kind of heavy object from the bedside table and smashes Shellard over the head with it."

Shellard is knocked unconscious but that is when Shirley goes to work.

She takes a needle and injects him with heroin as she wants to make everything look like an overdose.

Then they pulled down his pants.

"Shellard is starting to come to," Orange said. "Then they shove a suppository up his rectum. Oxycontin. This coupled with the heroin is a powerful mix as he has a heart condition. A knock on the head, a shot of heroin and some Oxycontin shoved up his ass killed the man."

Peter is left for dead as Shirley lets some time pass before she calls the police.

A BAD ACTRESS AND A PAIR OF BUNGLING CRIMINALS

Shirley then conjures up her best Meryl Streep act as she calls the police and tells them that she has found Shellard dead on the floor.

"He was into rough sex," she blubbered. "I don't know who could have done this to him."

Police arrived and found the dead Shellard with a towel covering his genitals. His ankles were handcuffed and he was wearing a mouth gag. He also had dog leads, electrical cords and ropes tied around him.

Unfortunately for Shirley, however, the two junkies she hired were not exactly professionals.

A fingerprint sweep led police to Sophia.

Her print had been found on a hallway telephone. They would also find her DNA on a partially smoked cigarette in the kitchen.

The police would track down Sophia as well as her junkie boyfriend. They both confessed to the crime.

"I did it," Stanley said the moment he took a seat in the interrogation room. "Well, I should say that I helped them do it. Shirley drove me and Sophia to the mansion. She wanted him tied up because he had forced her to do bondage with him. Bondage! The dude had frozen all her accounts and was trying to sell her house behind her back. She told him that she wanted to sign some papers so that she could get her house back."

Stanley described the evening of the killing as a casual night on the town. He stated that Shirley took Sophia and himself to a hotel for some gambling.

"We played the poker machines," Stanley told the police. "Then we got some heroin and went to the mansion. Shirley had a syringe of heroin. She went into his bedroom and stuck him with it."

Shellard's daughters, all decent young women, were in shock at what happened to her father. Shirley took it upon herself to try and comfort Jenny but didn't mince words about the kind of man he was.

"Your father was into bondage," Shirley said to her after she tried to sell the police on the fact that Shellard's death was likely due to rough sex. "We never hurt each other, though."

"After my dad died, I confided in Shirley for support," Jenny said. "I thought that she would be the only one who could possibly understand the pain I was going through because she was going through it too."

Shirley didn't know that while she was talking daily on the phone with Jenny, the police had her phone tapped.

They would find out that Shirley was calling around asking for a hitman.

Setting up a sting, they assigned an undercover officer for the operation.

A HITMAN COMETH

Shirley made it known that she was looking for someone to "off" both Sophia and Stanley, thereby getting rid of her only witnesses.

An undercover officer, code-named "Victor" called Shirley and set up four meetings.

"Can you get me pictures of them?" Victor asked.

"No," Shirley said. "But I can get you their address."

"What do they do for a living?"

"They don't 'do' anything," Shirley scoffed. "They're fucking junkies. They sit around all day and shoot heroin."

"Why do you want them killed?"

"They were responsible for killing my husband," Shirley said. "I want them both taken care of."

"It will cost you ten thousand dollars," Victor said. "I need three grand up front. Down payment."

"No problem."

"I need you to get as specific as you can," the hitman said. "Do you want it to be quick or do you want them to suffer?"

"Yes," Shirley said, her eyes cold.

"But do you want them dead?" the hitman asked again. "Or in a wheelchair for the rest of their lives?"

"I want them both dead," Shirley said with finality. "Dead."

Shirley would be arrested and charged with Shellard's murder while the two junkies would receive six years in jail for manslaughter.

In 2007, however, Shirley would elect to go to trial. In her appeal, she somehow convinced the judge that she didn't mean to kill Shellard. She only meant to teach him a lesson.

Shirley would be sentenced to thirteen years in prison which could be lessened to nine years with good behavior.

At the time of this writing, Shirley has become eligible for parole.

A FINAL BETRAYAL

The story took another turn for the bizarre when trustees of Vera Moore's estate would claim that millions of dollars that Moore gave Shellard were meant as a loan and not a gift.

They argued that it should be repaid.

Moore had died eight years prior to Shellard being murdered. He had been a good friend of her son, Kenneth, who died in a car crash in 1972.

Moore then took a shine to the young Shellard, treating him as if he were her own son.

She would give him her son's Waring Bros Tourer Rolls-Royce. In return, Shellard would keep the elderly widow company. He would take her out of her suburban nursing home and drive her around in the Rolls-Royce while they would go out for tea.

"By all accounts," Orange said. "He seemed to have been good to her. Like a son. He was soon given the power of attorney for her and looked after her financial affairs."

Shellard would purchase the Rosecraddock mansion in 1984 for $1.4 million. This was done with Moore's money as the title was split between her company, Brenchley Gardens, and Shellard's company then called "Landro."

Shellard would always seem to have bad luck with women, not only while alive but in death as well as even the attorneys for his mother figure in Vera Moore would turn on him.

KATHERINE KNIGHT

CARL KEITH

63

Katherine Mary Knight was born to shed blood. Born October 24th, 1955, she has the distinction of being the first Australian woman to be sentenced to life without the possibility of parole when she murdered her de facto husband John Charles Thomas Price, born 6 January 1955, in Aberdeen, New South Wales, Australia. The murder itself is not necessarily the stuff of horror films or nightmares with extreme heinousness even though Knight did, in fact, stab Price 37 times. Knight's subsequent defilement of Price's body following the murder was extremely atrocious and, as such, was the fundamental reason she received a life without parole sentence. So heinous, in fact that her file is marked "never to be released."

After stabbing Price to death, Knight proceeded to utilize her career skills as a butcher in an abattoir (slaughterhouse) to expertly and precisely excise Price's skin from his corpse in one piece which she hung from a meat hook inside an archway of the house before decapitating him and boiling his head with some vegetables for dinner. She also cut pieces from the victim's buttocks and cooked those as well, making two dinner plates with vegetables for Price's children. As a result, Knight is often referred to among Australians as the "Black Knight" and Aberdeen—once a charming small community named for Aberdeen, Scotland, located approximately 266 kilometers north-northwest of Sydney with a population slightly less than 1,800 that was known for its picturesque countryside, abattoirs, and as the birthplace of the blue heeler cattle dog—is now permanently blemished by Katherine Knight and her heinous crime.

Early Life

Knight was born at Tenterfield Hospital in Aberdeen, New South Wales, Australia, to Barbara Roughan (nee Thorley) who already had four boys—Patrick, Martin, Neville, and Barry—from a prior marriage and another son, Charlie, with her current lover and Katherine's father Ken Knight, an abattoir slaughterman. Barbara was forced to move to another town following cultivating a relationship with Ken, one of her then-husband's co-workers. This relationship was a scandal because of both families' renown within the town. At the time, Jack Roughan had four children and while his two older ones stayed with him and Barbara, the two younger ones were sent to Sydney to live with an aunt. Barbara then gave birth to twins Katherine and Joy, with Joy a half an hour older than Katherine. When the twins were four, Jack died and his two older children moved in with the Knights.

Knight had a troubling upbringing, to say the least. Due to her maternal great-grandmother's Aboriginal heritage and the overwhelming racism in the area at that time, the resulting tension was difficult for all of the children. As a result, Knight was a relatively isolated child; the only people with whom she was close were her twin sister and her Uncle Oscar Knight who, tragically, committed suicide in 1969. Following this heartbreak, the Knights moved back to Aberdeen.

Compounding her isolation, Knight had to contend with an alcoholic father who resorted to intimidation and violence regularly. It is reported that Ken would sexually assault Barbara as many as ten times per day. Barbara shared intimate details of her sex life and her contempt for men and sex with both Katherine and Joy. Further—as if the aforementioned was not enough—Knight claimed repeated sexual abuse by several family members (not her father, though) until she was 11 years old. Despite psychiatrists believing that this did occur, specific details are in doubt. Nonetheless, it is generally widely-accepted that she did suffer said abuse.

Amidst all of this turmoil in her life, everyone who knew her as a child said that while Knight was a generally pleasant girl who earned recognition and awards for her good behavior she did experience uncontrollable rages in response to seemingly minor upsets. During her high school years at Muswellbrook High School she was remembered by former classmates as a bully who attacked at least one student with a weapon and also assaulted a teacher who, in self-defense, injured Knight.

Knight ultimately left school at 15, virtually illiterate. She was, however, able to obtain employment in a clothing factory as a fabric cutter. One year later, at the age of 18, she began working at the local abattoir where her job was to decapitate the pigs; something in which she took great interest and pleasure, often watching the pigs having their throats slit before they reached her. Whereas some of her coworkers thought her behavior to be rather macabre, they just chalked it up to her taking an interest in all aspects of her employer's function. Soon thereafter she secured what she called her "dream job" as an offal (animal organs) cutter at the abattoir. Not long after this Knight was promoted to boner and given her very own set of razor-sharp butcher knives; what she called her most prized possessions. Knight—at every place she ever lived—hung her knives on a nail above her bed so, according to her, they "would always be handy if [she] needed them."

When one, after the fact, examines Knight's early life there are many indications that she would have likely snapped and resorted to murder. If people would have not chalked her erratic behavior up to her "normal" state and reported her disturbing behavior perhaps much of her mayhem could have been prevented.

A Series of Failed Relationships

David Kellett

Knight met her first husband, 22-year old truck driver and hard-drinking David Stanford Kellett in 1973 and as soon as Knight turned 18 she moved in with him. The relationship was one where Knight wore the proverbial pants. If Kellett got into a fight due to his drinking, Knight would be there to use her fists, if necessary, to back him up. In fact, throughout Aberdeen Knight was known for "offering armed combat to anyone who upset her."

Despite her domination of him, Kellett agreed to marry Knight in 1974—at her request. Her mother told Kellett on their wedding day that he had better watch Knight "or she'll fuc*ing kill you." She warned him that if he said or did the wrong thing, cheated on her, or otherwise stirred her up that Knight would not hesitate to kill him. Barbara also told Kellett that her daughter had "a screw loose somewhere." He didn't have to wait long to find this out for himself. On their wedding night after Kellett fell asleep after having sex with Knight only three times, she tried to strangle him for failing to perform to her expectations.

Things progressed from bad to worse with a pregnant Knight burning all of Kellett's clothing and shoes before assaulting him with a frying pan to the back of his head after he came home late from a darts competition at a local pub. Kellett sustained a fractured skull from the altercation and while he initially wanted to press charges against her, Knight—in her loving, best behavior—got him to change his mind. In fact, Kellett was so afraid of his wife that he secretly sought medical care the following day at work.

In May 1976 Knight gave birth to the couple's first child; a daughter named Melissa Ann. Shortly thereafter Kellett tired of Knight's possessiveness and domineering, violent behavior and left her for another woman. The pair fled to Queensland which, as would be expected, did not sit well with his wife. The next day, Knight was seen violently pushing Melissa in a pram down the main street, shaking it roughly from side to side and also stole an axe from a neighbor's back yard and swung it about her head threatening to kill random people. Subsequently, Knight was admitted into St. Elmo's Hospital in Tamworth where she received a diagnosis of postpartum depression. She remained in the hospital for several weeks. Shortly after her release, she left two-month old Melissa on railway tracks soon before a train was expected to arrive. If it wasn't for a homeless man who was known around town as "Old Ted" foraging near the tracks and who heard Melissa crying, the baby would have been killed. Arrested for her negligence, Knight was sent back to St. Elmo's but signed herself out the following day.

Within a week Knight cut the face of local teenager 16-year old Margaret Macbeth with one of her precious knives and ordered the woman to drive her to Queensland to find Kellett. Macbeth escaped when they stopped at a service station and by the time police arrived Knight was threatening a small boy she had taken hostage with her knife. Police disarmed her by attacking her with brooms and she was subsequently admitted into the Morisset Psychiatric Hospital where she told anyone who would listen to her how she was frequently abused by Kellett. She also informed the nurses that she was planning to kill the service station mechanic because he had fixed Kellett's car which then allowed him to leave with his new girlfriend. Knight added that she had planned to murder both Kellett and his mother when she reached Queensland.

After finding out about his wife's plans and disturbing behavior Kellett left his new girlfriend and he and his mother moved to Aberdeen to take care of Knight who was released on 9 August 1976 into their care. Knight, Kellett, and Kellett's mother subsequently moved to Woodridge, a suburb of Brisbane, where Knight was overjoyed to find work at the Dinmore Meatworks in nearby Ipswich.

Shortly thereafter, another example of her ability to attack without provocation involved a local police officer who Knight stabbed but—as was the case with every prior assault—she was never charged. Kellett also recounted another incident wherein he awakened one morning to find Knight straddling his chest grazing his throat with one of her knives. He said that she just laughed at him and stated how easy it would have been for her to kill him. An informative omen, to say the least.

Despite all of the disturbing behavior Knight displayed, Kellett got her pregnant again and on 6 March 1980 little Natasha Maree was born; however, in 1984 the marriage completely disintegrated due to Knight's constant jealousy of Kellett's truck driving job and relentless allegations of his having girlfriends everywhere and she ultimately left him, moving in with her parents back in Aberdeen for a short while before renting a house on McQueen Street in nearby Muswellbrook where she returned to her prior job at the abattoir. Kellett learned of this by returning home from work one night to an empty house.

In 1985, Knight injured her back and was subsequently placed on disability where she received a disability pension. Soon thereafter, Knight again moved back to Aberdeen where she and her daughters lived in a Housing Commission house.

David Saunders

In 1986, Knight met 38-year old divorced miner David Saunders who, a few months after that, moved in with Knight and her daughters while simultaneously maintaining his own apartment in Scone. Saunders was smitten with Knight even knowing full well that she had several "shortcomings" such as attacking people with kitchen appliances, knives, and her fists, but he could not overlook the fact that she was cheerful and charming and possessed a voracious sexual appetite. As would be expected, Knight was extremely jealous about why he kept his apartment and accused him repeatedly of cheating on her. Knight repeatedly threw Saunders out of the house and he returned to Scone each time. Invariably she would seek him out and beg him to come back, which he did.

In May 1987 Knight slit the throat of Saunders' two-month old dingo puppy in front of him as an example of what she would do to him if he ever cheated on her. She then hit Saunders in the head with a frying pan, knocking him unconscious.

Not unlike Kellett, despite all of Knight's violence and unpredictability, in June of the following year, Knight gave birth to Saunders' and her daughter Sarah. Saunders put a deposit on a house that Knight paid off in 1989 with her workers' compensation settlement. Disturbingly, Knight heavily decorated the family house with animal pelts, skulls, leather jackets and old boots, machetes, rusty animal traps, horns, rakes, and pitchforks. And as usual, her butchering knives were hung on the wall above the de facto marital bed.

Another altercation between Knight and Saunders occurred that resulted in Knight hitting Saunders in the face with an iron prior to stabbing him in the stomach with scissors. Of course, he moved back to his Scone apartment during which time Knight had cut up all of his clothes; something he discovered upon his return. She also vandalized his car and attempted suicide by overdosing on sleeping pills which led to her being admitted into yet another psychiatric hospital. This was the last straw and, subsequently, Saunders took a long leave of absence from work and went into hiding. Knight tried to find him but nobody admitted to her whether or not he or she knew where Saunders was. When he tried to return to visit his daughter, Knight had already reported to the police that she was afraid of him and was issued an Apprehended Violence Order (AVO)—similar to a restraining order in the United States—against him.

John Chillingworth

In 1990, Knight became pregnant by 43-year old abattoir worker—and her former coworker—John Chillingworth. In 1991 she gave birth to a boy named Eric. Not surprisingly, from the beginning of their relationship volatility ensued. Chillingworth, a recovering alcoholic, did admit that he struck Knight once after she had pushed him too far after hitting him in the face, knocking his glasses off his face and breaking his dentures in his mouth. Their relationship lasted three more years before she left him for yet another man; a man with whom she had been having an affair for some time: John Price.

John Price

John "Pricey" Price already had three children when he met and began an affair with Knight. He was very well-liked and everyone who knew him described him as a "terrific bloke" whose own marriage ended in 1988. He had custody of his two older children while their then-two-year old daughter went to live with his ex-wife. Even though

Price was well aware of Knight's volatile reputation he still began an affair with her and in 1995 she and her children moved into his house. As was the case with all of her relationships, Price's and hers started out great; he had a steady, well-paying job in the local mines and her children liked him. However, their violent arguments—often precipitated by excessive alcohol consumption—intensified.

In 1998, Knight and Price argued because he refused to marry her so, in true retaliatory Katherine Knight form, she exacted revenge by videotaping items he had allegedly stolen from work and subsequently sending the tape to his boss. Even though the items consisted of out-of-date first aid kits that he found in the company's trash dumpster, Price was fired from the job he had worked for 17 years. Logically, Price kicked Knight out of his house and as she moved back to her own house the news of her actions quickly spread throughout the sleepy town.

Not unlike Knight's former lovers, Price couldn't stay away from her. Despite her horrible temper and violent streak, when she was loving and kind she was the perfect partner. Even though they restarted their relationship he refused to permit her to move back into his house. Of course, the fighting intensified because Knight did not have complete control over him. Additionally, because of his choice to continue to be with her Price lost many of his friends and acquaintances who refused to have anything to do with him while they were together.

In February 2000, Knight's assaults on Price increased, culminating with her stabbing him in the chest. Again, he kicked her out of his house and on 29 February he stopped by the Scone Magistrate Court on his way to work and took out an AVO on Knight—actually after discussing his fears with Knight's first husband, David Kellett—to keep her away from both him and his children. Price was able to secure new employment with Bowditch and Partners Earth Moving and was promoted to supervisor after 12 months and told his boss and coworkers that afternoon that if he failed to come to work the next day to expect that Knight had killed him. Despite his coworkers and boss urging him to not go back to her—even offering to let him stay with them—his worry for his children made him decline their gracious invitations. This would be the worst decision of his life.

When Price arrived home, his children were gone as Knight sent them to a friend's house for a sleepover. He spent a relaxing evening with the neighbors before retiring for the night at approximately 11:00 p.m. Knight arrived at Price's house later that night with the brand new black lingerie she had purchased earlier that day. Also earlier that day, Knight had videotaped herself singing nursery rhymes and hugging and kissing her children while making strange comments; the tape would later be referred to as some type of crude will in which she talked about hoping to be able to see them again. At Price's house, Knight watched television, took a shower, and climbed into his bed where she awakened him and the two of them had sex. Price fell back asleep afterward.

The Crime

Price was awakened by the first of 37 stab wounds Knight inflicted upon him with one of her prized, razor-sharp butcher knives. According to autopsy results, many of the wounds punctured vital organs. Blood evidence at the scene demonstrates that Price did, in fact, attempt to escape from Knight's attack and he actually managed to get to the front door—being repeatedly stabbed the entire time—before he was dragged back into the hallway where he finally exsanguinated and perished.

As if the brutal murder was not enough, what Knight did after Price died was extremely heinous and unbelievable.

After Price was dead, Knight skinned his body and hung the pelt—completely intact—from a meat hook through the head above an archway in his house. Interestingly, she left a small, one-inch square of skin intact upon his body that contained a scar from where she had previously stabbed him. Knight's skinning of Price's skin was so expertly done that following his autopsy, it was able to be reattached to his body in a manner indicative of a clear and appropriate methodology; thus underscoring Knight's adeptness due to her years of experience in the abattoir, likely coupled with her macabre fascination with knives, death, and similar topics.

She then decapitated him and placed his skinned head in a big stock pot on the stove with vegetables. The pot was still warm when police arrived the following morning. Knight also cooked parts of Price—later identified as his buttocks—and served them up as "steak" on two plates with zucchini, squash, cabbage, pumpkin, potatoes, and gravy atop the dinner table. Each plate had beside it a spiteful note for each of Price's children. Knight, apparently, was going to serve the children their own father for dinner. Another "meal" was found in the back yard with some speculating that it was for the dog and others conjecturing that Knight intended to consume parts of her lover but could not bring herself to eat it and discarded it.

She then returned to Price's headless and skinless corpse and arranged his body on the floor with his left arm resting atop an empty 1.25-liter Shelley's Club Lemon Squash soft drink bottle, his legs crossed, and a blood-stained, 31-centimeter yellow plastic-handled knife that matched the type of knife used to commit the heinous act by his right hand.

She also left a handwritten, blood-stained and flesh-covered note atop a picture of Price that read, "*Time you got back Johnathon for rapping [raping] my douter [daughter]. You to Beck [Price's daughter] for Ross—for Little John [Price's son]. Now play with little Johns Dick John Price.*" [sic] What Knight hoped to accomplish by penning this note is unknown and all of the accusations were proven to be baseless.

Knight has repeatedly claimed that she has no memory of what happened that fateful night after she and Price had sex.

Price's neighbor became concerned that his work vehicle was still in his driveway at 6:00 a.m. the following morning. Similarly, Price's employer was worried when he failed to arrive at work and sent a coworker to check on him. When the two men saw blood on the front door they called the police who arrived at Price's house at approximately 8:00 a.m. When police entered the house they were met with a grisly crime scene and discovered Knight on the bed comatose from attempting suicide with sleeping pills. After she had killed him, Knight drove to an Aberdeen ATM and withdrew $1,000 from Price's account and then swallowed the pills.

The police officers who found the macabre crime scene at 84 Andrews Street in Aberdeen testified that Knight had skinned Price so methodically that his entire skin—including face, ears, scalp, neck, and even his genitals—was completely intact and resembled that of a "macabre suit" only someone with her abattoir knowledge could achieve. Detective Senior Constable Peter Anthony Muscio issued the complete report that detailed the condition of Price's body, the tremendous amount of blood spatter and pooling throughout the house which indicated that Price did, in fact, fight vehemently for his life, and the gruesome discovery in the kitchen.

The crime scene was so disturbing, so utterly distressing, that many experienced police officers and forensic personnel assigned to the crime scene took stress leave soon after the investigation was completed. Some even admit to still suffering from elements of posttraumatic stress disorder suffered as a result. Even Knight's first husband, Kellett, admitted that he cried for days thinking about what she did and this was compounded by the fact that he had met and spoken to Price shortly before his demise. Kellett still fears for his life even though Knight will never be free again.

The Trial

Knight initially offered to plead guilty to manslaughter and, rightfully, was rejected. She was arraigned on 2 February 2001 for murder to which she pled not guilty. The trial was originally to commence on 23 July 2001 but was later reset for 15 October 2001 due to her attorney's illness. When the trial began, Justice Barry O'Keefe offered to excuse any of the 60 potential jurors who so desired due to the extremely graphic and disturbing photographic evidence that would be brought up during the trial. Five accepted. Several more asked to be excused when the witness list was revealed. Judge O'Keefe adjourned the trial after being informed that Knight wanted to change her plea to guilty and ordered a psychiatric evaluation that night to determine whether Knight understood the ramifications of a guilty plea and was legally sane to do so. Whereas Knight's attorneys initially planned to offer a defense of amnesia and dissociation—which the majority of psychiatrists supported—she was found to be legally sane despite what some psychiatrists thought to be the dominance of her primitive conscience; one that was ruled by the violence, incest, pedophilia, and rape that permeated her childhood. Knight had experienced more sex and violence than love throughout her life and the former dominated her relationships with others, particularly men. The speculation surrounding this proposed defense strategy was that Knight attempted to eat part of Price but the abhorrence she experienced caused her to dissociate from reality and to block everything out of her memory.

The next morning Knight changed her plea to guilty and the empaneled jury was dismissed. As there was no reason given why Knight changed her plea, it was speculated that when confronted with the horror of what she did when shown the crime scene photographs she wanted to spare jurors the similar horror of having to hear all of the gruesome details.

There is much comment in the literature that those who saw Knight sitting at the defense table admitted that she did not look like the vindictive monster that she truly was. It was well-known that she was not someone to cross and ex-lovers and family members testified at her trial that Knight was someone fully capable of considerable violence, even though when not in a murderous rage Knight was the perfect mother and housewife. Chillingworth testified about the incident where Knight killed his puppy and the story of how she got Price fired over an alleged stolen first aid kit was also introduced. Once all of the witnesses were finished testifying the general consensus was that her looks were not to be taken as fact and that someone far more dangerous lurked beneath her seemingly calm exterior. Knight's over-the-top mental and physical vindictiveness demonstrated—to many experts—her vehement belief in revenge and an overdeveloped sense of entitlement. She was also described as one who delighted in making people afraid of her and that she was incapable of true love and empathy as she did not receive either as a developing child. Additional speculation suggested that Knight had fantasized about killing a human being for years and when she did, took considerable pride in her "work"—her ultimate "triumph."

Once Price went to see the police to obtain an AVO against Knight, prosecutors argued that at this moment she put her murderous plot into motion as evidenced by purchasing new lingerie to wear while she seduced him, ensuring that her knives were sharp enough, and making sure that she had the right pots handy for his head. Psychiatrists and criminal profilers asserted that she derived great pleasure from the planning and her subsequent action.

At her trial, one of Australia's foremost criminal psychologists, Dr. Rod Milton, presented his findings following Knight's interview and asserted that she suffered from borderline personality disorder. Borderline personality disorder is a serious mental illness responsible for mood instability, unstable behavior, and typically stormy relationships. It usually affects more women and begins during adolescence or early adulthood. Those who suffer from the disorder commonly have serious problems regulating thoughts and emotions, act impulsively and oftentimes recklessly, and experience very unstable relationships—all of these traits occurred in droves with Knight. Additional symptoms prevalent in individuals with borderline personality disorder include fear of abandonment; an unstable self-image or confused self-identity; self-damaging behaviors such as excessive spending, promiscuity, substance abuse, reckless driving, or binge eating; self-injury or suicidal behavior or ideations; very random and often violent mood swings; a constant feeling of sadness or worthlessness; anger problems to include frequent loss of temper and/ or physical altercations; and paranoia or loss of contact with reality. Those who knew Knight would likely say that she possessed virtually every single one of these qualities. Her extreme fear of abandonment led to her volatile temper and resultant physically violent behavior with her lovers, she attempted suicide on several occasions, her mood swings were frequent and severe, she was very promiscuous which led to her affairs and constant attempts to seduce lovers who had kicked her out, and she regularly consumed a considerable amount of alcohol. Experts link extreme fear of abandonment to the release of adrenaline and norepinephrine which likely account for the trademark severe mood swings and angry outbursts and Knight's continual fear of abandonment and accusations that her lovers were cheating on her resulted in an inordinate amount of these neurotransmitters coursing through her body.

Borderline personality disorder is believed to be an illness with both biological and environmental influences. Heredity and childhood abuse—particularly sexual abuse—have been theorized to be among the strongest predictors of whether someone has a greater predisposition to developing the disorder. Further, the brains of those with borderline personality disorder demonstrate structural abnormalities and resulting malfunction which suggests that the illness has a biological foundation. More specifically, those areas of the brain responsible for emotions and feelings demonstrate higher than average brain activity.

The name borderline personality disorder was originally so named as sufferers were considered to be on the "borderline" between neurosis and psychosis with some professionals asserting that the name was inaccurate. With respect to Knight, that she has frequently been called psychotic may demonstrate some validity in this moniker. The fundamental differences between neuroses and psychoses are that while the former are mild mental disorders, the latter result from gross mental and emotional disruptions to include personality changes; lost or changed contact with reality; projection of certain thoughts upon others; loss of the ego to the id; disorganized, bizarre, and irrational thought processes; and frequent hospitalization due to attempted suicide and/or other self-harming behaviors. Whereas the literature suggests that individuals with borderline personality disorder experience some alleviation of their impulsivity and volatility when they reach their 40's, such was not the case with Knight.

Another speculation regarding Knight's psychological nature involves piquerism, defined as sexual arousal by cutting or stabbing another's skin, sometimes resulting in death. The literature defines piquerism as a form of paraphilic sadism which can range from a single prick, to multiple stab wounds to an eroticized area, to elaborate cutting, stabbing, or mutilation; with the last eerily similar to Knight's treatment of Price's deceased body. Piquerism is closely associated with so-called "lust murders" in which the offender stabs or mutilates the victim. Other common attributes associated with piquerism include posing or propping of the deceased's body, inserting items into various bodily cavities, anthropophagy (eating flesh or consuming blood), and necrophilia. Knight did, in fact, pose Price's corpse and planned to feed his flesh to his children and, perhaps, attempted to consume some herself. Prevalence of this disorder is currently unknown.

Sentencing

At her sentencing hearing on 9 November 2001, despite having pled guilty, Knight never accepted responsibility for her actions in Price's death. At this hearing, Knight's legal team requested her removal from the courtroom so she wouldn't have to listen to all of the details that she had allegedly forgotten which was adamantly denied and she was given the harshest sentence allowed under Australian law. When Dr. Timothy Lyons—the medical examiner who conducted Price's autopsy—took the stand and described every single gory detail, Knight became hysterical and required sedation.

According to Dr. Lyons, Price, thankfully, was already dead when he was skinned. The skinning was conducted professionally with the razor sharp knife inserted beneath his collarbone and sliced across to the other shoulder before being cut down Price's chest, over his stomach to his pubic area where a "T" was cut so the knife sliced down the front of his legs to his feet before moving the knife back up his body, skinning the back of his arms and the top of his head before peeling the victim's skin off in one piece, exposing his intestines. The skin displayed every single one of Knight's 37 stab wounds. Price's head was then removed with a clean cut at the C3-C4 juncture just above his shoulders. Dr. Lyons stated that the entire process would have taking approximately 40 minutes. Further, Dr. Lyons testified that the myriad wounds entered Price's aorta, both of his lungs, his liver, his stomach, his pancreas, his colon, and left kidney that had part of it completely sliced off.

Just prior to handing down Knight's sentence, Justice O'Keefe said of Price that *"The last minutes of his life must have been a time of abject terror for him as they were a time of utter enjoyment for her...she has not expressed any contrition or remorse and if released she poses a serious threat to the security of society."* Knight was given a life sentence without the possibility of parole and became the first woman in Australia's history with the distinction of having her file marked "never to be released." Of particular interest was that Australia had no statutory prohibition to the defilement Knight committed against Price's corpse which precluded her being charged with additional crimes. Her actions were so out of the scope of the law that it was likely unbelievable that someone could do something like this to another human being.

Evidence of her premeditation was further indicated when she said to one of Price's daughters "I told him if he took me back this time it was to the death."

Post-Conviction

In June 2006, Knight appealed her life sentence, asserting that life without the possibility of parole was too severe for murder; however a three-judge panel in the New South Wales Court of Criminal Appeal consisting of Justices Peter McClellan, Megan Latham, and Michael Adams dismissed her petition in September of that same year citing that her crime was so appalling and "almost beyond contemplation in a civilized society." Justice McClellan stated during her appeal that "*The psychiatric evidence indicates that her personality is unlikely to change in the future and, if released, she would be likely to inflict serious injury or perhaps death on others.*"

It has been alleged that Knight was inspired the horror film *Resurrection* (1999) in which a serial killer tried to reconstruct the body of Christ with parts of his victims. There is some speculation that Knight was a copycat of sorts of a gruesome scene in which a body was killed, decapitated, and then skinned and hung on a meat hook.

BLUE EYED BUTCHER : THE TRUE STORY OF SUSAN WRIGHT

ASHLEY GORMAN

The murder of Jeff Wright was one of the most brutal and controversial in Texas history. His wife, Susan Wright, stabbed him in excess of 193 times before burying his body in a shallow grave in the back of their home. What followed was a media frenzy as Susan was dubbed as the "Blue Eyed Butcher." Court TV televised the entire trial while numerous media outlets devoted special segments to the case.

But the picture didn't fit.

Susan was depicted as this cold-blooded, sadistic killer. Everyone who has met her, however, has come away feeling that she was a shy, polite woman who could not harm a fly. The prosecuting attorney would claim that her politeness was just an act...Was it an act? Or did Susan simply snap after being abused one time too many?

EARLY LIFE

There were three of the children altogether, Susan, Cindy and a brother named Jim. They were raised in an upper-middle-class home in Harris County. Susan's mother was a stay at home mom while her father was a mechanical engineer.

A shy and reserved child, Susan stated that she walked on eggshells at home as her father would abuse her mother.

"She was trained to put on a smile and make everything seem like it was all right," forensic psychologist Paula Orange said. "It became normal for her to see a father yelling at her mother and she thought it was something that went on in every household."

Susan's sister, Cindy, would maintain that Susan would have trouble standing up for herself. She tried out for the drill team and was berated by one of the older girls. Susan felt so violated that she transferred to another school.

Susan was a mediocre student in high school and made C's in the majority of her classes. She didn't date much but tried to get attention from boys. She had one boyfriend tell her she was "too fat" which prompted Susan to lose almost twenty pounds. At the age of eighteen, she had a boyfriend that told her to work as a topless dancer at a strip club called the Gold Cup.

She worked as a stripper there for about two months but grew tired of it, stating that the money wasn't worth it and that she did it to feel better about herself.

Susan then used the money to go a local community college where she enrolled in a nursing program. Still needing extra cash, she found began working as a hair stylist. She dropped out the nursing program just as fast as she quit exotic dancing, stating that the curriculum was too time-consuming and would cost too much.

"There are two ways to look at Susan's early life," Orange said. "One is to say that she was into the cocaine and fast lifestyle that the stripper scene would provide. The other is to say that perhaps she was looking for acceptance. Being a topless dancer is going to be judged harshly by adults. But to the young men she was trying to get attention from, it would be seen as something pretty cool."

Jeff Wright would see that something "pretty cool" in Susan the moment he laid eyes on her at a get together on Galveston Beach in Texas.

THE HANDSOME SUITOR

Jeff had been a notorious party animal in school. He enjoyed booze and cocaine but began thinking more about settling down as he turned thirty.

He then met the twenty-one-year-old Susan at the beach. She was a struggling waitress, he was a successful carpet and tile salesman. Smitten by her pretty face and blonde hair, he began pursuing her with vigor, showering Susan with expensive gifts and fancy dinners.

After a few months of dating, Susan announced that she was pregnant. Jeff would tell her that it would be "okay" if she got an abortion but they decided to keep the baby and marry instead. Susan, however, was upset that Jeff waited until she was eight months pregnant to propose.

A week after his proposal, the young couple exchanged vows in a small ceremony near Houston, Texas.

Susan would later claim that Jeffrey would change dramatically after the wedding night. He would taunt Susan, calling her a "fat ass" as she gained weight during the pregnancy. Susan became depressed after the baby was born and Jeff mocked her even further for seeing a doctor who diagnosed her with postpartum depression.

Jeff's controlling behavior got worse with time. He disallowed Susan to take the anti-depressants the doctor had prescribed her. He then began limiting the people she could have in her life, allowing Susan to see her mother but she could only be out of the house for an hour and a half. Susan wanted to take classes at a junior college but Jeff did not allow it. He then became infuriated when Susan went to the campus to enroll anyway, signing up for an Internet course. She had been gone out of the house too long, however, and Jeff became enraged.

"You nasty whore," he screamed as she entered the home. "Are you cheating on me?"

Jeff would smoke marijuana just about every day but according to Susan, the cannabis never took the edge off his personality. She found him to always be easily irritated as anything could set him off. He would complain about problems at work and the utility bills being too high. Then he would single out Susan for keeping a dirty house, fixing a lousy meal or not allowing the kids run around the house screaming.

APPEARANCES CAN BE DECEIVING

On the surface, both Jeff and Susan put on a false front that their home was a place of domestic bliss.

The couple purchased a home in the White Oaks subdivision in the Cypress-Fairbanks area of Houston. This was a fairly affluent area and Jeff was still doing well financially selling carpets and tiles. Another child followed, a daughter they named Kailey, and Susan kept house like a modern day June Cleaver. She entertained friends, family, and neighbors with parties and made sure that her home was the tidiest on the block. Susan had a level of perfectionism which she applied to her home life, she cooked and cleaned, making sure dinner was made and served at the exact same time each day.

Susan also tended the garden and flowers outside the home while Jeff dug out the porch and was in the process of installing a fountain.

Domestic life didn't sit well with Jeff. The cocaine addiction soon got the best of him.

"There were rumors about Jeff," forensic psychologist Paula Orange said. "That he would go to strip clubs and have threesomes with strippers."

Susan knew when Jeff was going on a binge as would become hyperactive, getting too rough with both her and the children. Susan would state that Jeff had kicked, punched and slapped her around during his cocaine-fueled episodes.

"This needs to stop," Susan said as Jeff bounced off the walls in rage.

"You don't fucking tell me what to do," Jeff said, his eyes bleary red. "I'm a grown ass man and you don't give me the rules. I make the fucking rules."

Susan ran to her room.

NO WAY OUT

In the summer of 1999, Jeff had physically beat Susan one night. Susan waited for him to leave the next morning then she packed her bags and took her children to her sister's home. Jeff called her later and told her that a delivery truck was coming by.

"Pack all your stuff back in there," Jeff hissed. "Because if you don't, I will kill you or Bradley."

Fearing for her life, Susan complied.

Jeff's aggression may have been fueled by his cocaine addiction which got the family into financial debt. He also began dating other women.

"He would go through an Internet dating site," Orange said. "He gave Susan herpes. She confronted him about it and he told her that if she 'was a better wife he wouldn't need other women.'"

The belittling and beatings became a daily occurrence as time wore on but Susan never called the police.

"That was a bit problem for the defense during her trial," Orange said. "There were so few people who saw the abuse take place. She had a neighbor who reported that Susan looked terrified of Jeff at times and another who said she saw Jeff grab her by the arm once. But there was never a police report of any kind of domestic disturbance."

Susan would later state that she did not believe in divorce because of her Christian beliefs and that she didn't want to embarrass her family.

But by September of 2002, the marriage was in shambles. Jeff had a new job and wasn't making as much money as before. His cocaine and alcohol addiction had gotten worse. On one occasion, he came home drunk and urinated on their daughter's bed. He then bought an air rifle and hit Susan with the butt of the gun. On New Year's day 2003, his first words to his wife to start off the new year were "Happy fucking New Year, bitch. That will be your last."

THE FINAL STRAW

On the night of January 13th, 2003, Jeff went on another cocaine binge. He then began rough-housing with Bradley, trying to show his young son some boxing moves he learned at the local gym. The horseplay got out of hand as Jeff hit Bradley hard in the face. The boy began to cry and Jeff panicked, fearing Susan would hear.

He waited, fully expecting Susan to come in and investigate.

Minutes passed, then Jeff settled down and laid on the couch, luxuriating in the final hours of his cocaine high.

Susan then came in and took the children to bed. Jeff watched a little television and looked to doze off as the cocaine comedown began.

But his spirits were perked up again when Susan entered the living room wearing nothing more than a silk bathrobe. The light behind her illuminated her curves.

Jeff looked at his young wife with his mouth open. He reached over for the remote and turned off the television, following her into the bedroom without saying a word.

"Susan had enough," Orange said. "She was powerless against the two-hundred twenty pound Jeff in a fight. So she used the one thing that she knew Jeff could not refuse. The one area in their life that she had the power. Sex."

Jeff couldn't help but smile when he entered the bedroom. Susan had gone for an all-out seduction.

Susan looked up at Jeff and smirked as she began lighting red candles around the room. He could not take his eyes off his younger wife as she reached over and pressed play on the CD.

Slow and sexy music filled the air. No words were needed.

Jeff gulped hard. The pleasure of the cocaine buzz and the anticipation of his wife's hot body against his was more than he could bear. Jeff let Susan take the lead in his drug haze and he soon found himself with his back on the bed, buck naked.

Taking a pair of his neck ties, Susan began tying Jeff's arms to the headboard.

"What are you doing, baby?" he asked.

"Shhhh," she whispered as she moved down to his ankles and tied them to the footboard.

Tied down and spread-eagled on the bed, Jeff watched as Susan took one of the candles off the table.

Then she poured the hot wax on his upper thigh.

"The fuck you doing!"

Then she poured the melting wax over his testicles.

"Yaaarrrrgh!" Jeff screamed. "What the fuck!"

He writhed against the knots around his wrists. Susan had done a good job tying him down.

The room was now dimly lit as only a few candle lights remained. Jeff squinted in the darkness as Susan straddled him.

She held up a knife.

"What are you doing!!"

Jeff struggled against the knots again. Susan had done a good job of tying him up. She was a perfectionist.

She did a damn good job.

Jeff felt her take his penis in her hand, pressing the point of the blade against it with the other.

"The hell are you doing?" he screamed, his heart beating out of his chest.

"I've been way too nice to you," Susan said with calm authority. "I played the role of the meek housewife. I let you do what you want. Let you say whatever you want to me. But now, I'm tired. And it's time to turn the tables."

Susan nicked the blade across Jeff's penis.

Screams filled the air.

Susan then placed the point of the blade into his scrotum.

Jeff writhed and pulled against the knots. He could not free himself from the restraints around his wrists and ankles.

Susan then mounted him again and he saw the fiery evil in her eyes.

"Susan," he pleaded. "Please don't."

She stabbed Jeff in the eye first. Then his face and neck.

"She absolutely hated the man," Orange said. "She wanted to completely obliterate his face. It was an act of destruction where she completely wanted to remove his face."

Jeff screamed in pain. Susan began crying and screaming herself, a mixture of a battle cry and years of abuse breaking free. She screamed at Jeff, telling him about every wrong and act of abuse he threw her way.

Susan shrieked as she blitzed Jeff's body with the blade.

Jeff yelped in pain.

All the yelling, however, awoke Bradley.

He knocked on the door.

Susan quickly put on her bathrobe and walked the little boy back to his room.

"Why was daddy screaming?"

"Mommy and daddy are playing a game," Susan said. "Now you get some sleep."

After tucking Bradley back into bed, Susan went back to the bedroom.

Jeff, bloodied from over fifty knife wounds, was still alive.

"None of his wounds," Orange said. "Would have been enough to kill Jeff on its own. So he was laying there in excruciating pain, bleeding out.

Susan then got a second knife from the kitchen, a butcher knife. She returned to the bedroom and resumed her attack, stabbing Jeff another 140 times. The majority were to his face and neck but she attacked his genitals as well.

Tired from the stabbing, Susan caught her breath, waiting for the adrenaline to subside.

"He deserved it," she whispered to herself, trying to rationalize her actions.

Her mind in a fog, she walked over to the bedroom light and flicked it on.

Blood seeped through the bedsheets and was splattered across the walls.

Blood everywhere.

Susan shuddered with panic. There was no way in hell she could clean this mess up.

But she had to survive...And get away with the crime.

She began breaking things down, step by step. The first chore was to go into the shower and get cleaned up. She watched as Jeff's blood dripped off her and into the drain, her thoughts gathering.

Time to cover my ass, she thought, staring at her reflection in the fogged up bathroom mirror.

She then called Jeff's parents who lived over three hours away in Austin. Susan went into melodrama mode as the tears poured out.

"Susan?" Jeff's mother asked. "What is it?"

"It's Jeff," Susan said. "He came home from his boxing lessons and just went wacko."

"What do you mean?"

"He started hitting me," Susan sobbed. "Started hitting Bradley."

"Oh God, no. That's not Jeff."

"He wouldn't stop."

"Put Jeff on the phone."

"He's not here," Susan said. "He just ran out of the house. He's gone for good this time. I know it."

"What was he so angry about?"

"He's on drugs," Susan said. "Has been for a long, long time. Cocaine. Marijuana. Now he has no money and we're in debt because of it. He was just so frustrated all the time but tonight…. Tonight he just went wacko."

"Jeff doesn't do drugs."

"Yes," Susan nodded. "He can't help it. It's a secret."

Susan then remained on the phone with Jeff's parents for over an hour. They tried to console her as she detailed all of his abuses. Finally, she hung up and realized that she had to take care of his body.

But how?

After a few moments, she thought of the fountain out by the back porch. Jeff had left the job unfinished, as per usual, but the hole was pre-dug!

Her adrenaline still pumping, Susan went into the garage and retrieved a dolly that the couple used earlier to roll some new furniture into the house. She untied Jeff's body and plopped him onto the dolly, rolling him down the hall and dropping him face first in the shallow grave next to the back porch.

Another problem arose, however, as Jeff's body had begun to stiffen from the rigor mortis. She bent his legs and torso as much as she could to make him fit in the shallow hole. Then she began pouring the dirt over him.

It would be morning soon and she hurried back into the house. Susan mopped up the blood, starting from the patio, down the hallway and then to the bedroom itself. She rolled up the bloody bed sheets, gagging from the gruesome sight, then placed them into large Hefty bags.

Susan then pulled the mattress from the bed and dragged it into the backyard as she didn't know how to go about cleaning it just yet.

THE NEXT DAY

The children awoke early and Susan took them to daycare. She then drove to the hardware store and purchased a couple gallons of paint.

Arriving back at the house, Susan fought through fatigue and began to clean. She painted the walls and bleached out the blood on the carpet.

After a few hours, everything looked neat and tidy except for a bleach stain on the carpet.

Jeff's parents worried about their son. In the afternoon, they called Susan and asked if Jeff had come back home.

"He came by," Susan said. "Got his stuff and left."

"What do you mean 'got his stuff and left'?"

"He got some clothes," Susan paused, trying to get her story straight. "We started fighting again. He started yelling at me. Got a bottle of bleach and began pouring it around our bedroom. I thought he was going to set the place on fire."

"He wouldn't do that."

"He did," Susan said, adamant.

"We need to talk to him."

"He left his cell phone here," Susan said.

After the next few hours, Susan would field calls from Jeff's employer and a neighbor. She told Jeff's boss that he had gone "wacko" and told the neighbor the same story she had told Jeff's parents.

The neighbor advised Susan to call the police.

Susan realized that the noose around her neck would close fast if she didn't do something. She had to take the initiative somehow to get ahead of the investigation as Jeff's parents and the police would have plenty of questions.

First, she went to the emergency room and reported that she had been beaten by Jeff.

The doctor on duty at the time, Stephen Fischer, stated that he believed Susan and told her to report the injuries to the police. Later, under cross-examination, the prosecutor got Dr. Fischer to admit that he really didn't know how Susan got those injuries and was going strictly off what he told her.

On January 15th, 2003, two days after she had murdered Jeff, Susan entered Precinct Four of the Harris County Constable's office. She filed a report on Jeff, once again using the same story that she had told his parents and her neighbor.

She had physical evidence to back up her story as she had cuts on her hands and a bruise on her thigh.

"I'm scared of what will happen when he comes back," Susan informed the reporting officer. "He's abusive and violent."

A restraining order against Jeff was filed.

"She had a bruise on her thigh," Orange said. "The police chalked up her complaint as a routine domestic violence case."

A WEB OF DECEIT

Three days later, however, Susan felt the pressure of her lies. Jeff's parents kept calling, family and friends, plus his employer.

There was no way she could keep up this charade.

Looking out the window, she saw their dog, a chow mix, had dug up the area where Jeff had been buried. She could see the dog had unearthed Jeff's arm as well as the back of his head.

The chow had tried to pull its owner from its burial place, however, and in doing so had bitten off Jeff's hand.

The dog played with the hand as if it were a toy, laying it on the patio.

It was a sick irony, as Jeff would often beat the dog and once threw it against the wall.

But the visual of her husband's half-buried body and dismembered hand sent Susan into a panic.

She needed to tell someone.

Susan placed her daughter Kailey and son Bradley into her car and headed straight toward her mother's house.

She told her mother the same story as before, informing her about the restraining order.

"He'll kill me if he comes back," Susan said. Her voice was now half-hearted. She had to tell someone. If she was going to come clean, it would have to be with her mother first.

"Susan, you really need to tell me what's going on."

"It wasn't just a fight," Susan said to her mother, fighting back tears. "And he didn't just run away."

"What do you mean?"

"He's dead."

"You're overreacting."

"No," Susan said. " I stabbed him. I buried him in the backyard. I didn't know what else to do."

Susan slumped forward and put her head on the table, sobbing.

Her mother called Susan's sister Cindy to come pick up the children. She then had to save her daughter at all costs, calling up numerous defense attorneys to price them accordingly.

Her mother hired Neal Davis, who came to the home. He then informed the police of Jeff's body in the back yard.

The police searched the home and found evidence of blood that Susan had failed to clean during her bleach wash.

THE TRIAL

The case took over thirteen months to reach a trial which started on February 24th, 2004.

Susan would stake the stand and claim self-defense.

"Susan had a rough go of it in the trial," Orange said. "Every part of it was televised and she was going up against a prosecuting attorney named Kelly Siegler. Siegler was ferocious and often used out of the box methods to defeat defense attorneys."

Once the trial began, Siegler immediately pounced on Susan like Mike Tyson trying to finish his foe in the first few seconds of a fight.

The first question Siegler asked Susan was "Have you ever lied to avoid getting into trouble?"

"No," Susan said in an unsure voice "I can't say I ever have."

"Siegler's tactic was to show Susan to be the liar she was," Orange said. "Everyone on the jury has lied before. Show right off the bat, the prosecution hit a home run."

"He attacked me with a knife," Susan said. "He kept yelling 'Die, bitch! Die bitch!'"

"Why did you stab him almost 200 times?" the prosecutor asked.

"Once I started," Susan began to cry. "I couldn't stop. If I stopped, he would have killed me."

Siegler then called Susan's tears "fake." She argued that Susan killed Jeff in order to collect on a $200,000 life insurance policy.

Siegler then had the Wright's actual bed brought into the courtroom. The prosecutor asked a younger male member of her staff to lay on the bed while she re-enacted the murder for the jury. The man struggled against the restraints much like Jeff would have. Siegler then proceeded to "stab the victim" over and over again...197 times...stimulating Susan's act down to the very last stroke of the blade.

The jury was shaken by this visual. They would deliberate over five and a half-hours before declaring that Susan was guilty of murder.

"She stabbed Jeff at least 197 times," Orange said. "I say at least 197 times because the coroners determined that she stabbed him in numerous spots more than once. They couldn't determine the exact amount."

Susan's married life had echoed what she saw in her own childhood when she witnessed her mother go through nightly beat downs at the hands of her father. Susan's mother would later deny this but Susan's sister, Cindy, would confirm that their mother was indeed the victim of abuse. Cindy had a Ph.D., in psychology and would state that witnessing these beatings left a scar in Susan's memories that she could never erase.

"She stabbed Jeff for all the times that he punched her in the chest, and she stabbed him for all of the times that he raped her in the middle of the night. And she stabbed Jeff because he was just like her father."

In March of 2004, Susan would be sentenced to 25 years to left for killing Jeff Wright.

Things took a turn in her favor, however, when Misty McMichael came forward and relayed her experience with Jeff Wright. McMichael was another former stripper who had dated Jeff for four years and verified that she had been the victim of his violence and abuse.

The Fourteenth Court of Appeals of Texas then gave Susan a new hearing.

A video recording of Bradley was brought in as evidence for the new trial. Bradley was filmed in 2003 by Harris County Child Protective Services when he was four-years-old. In the video, Bradley was working on a coloring book.

"Have you ever seen your dad hit your mom?" the interviewer asked.

"No," Bradley said.

"Did you ever see bruises on your mom?"

"She has some on her legs."

"How did she get them?"

"I don't know."

The prosecution would later try to insinuate that Susan had drugged Jeff, noting the level of GHB (the 'date rape' drug) in her system. The toxicology report would reveal had Jeff had used cocaine but less than .1 gram was in his body. There was also 33 mg of GHB found but this is a naturally occurring chemical which exacerbates as the body decomposes. The toxicologist could only say there was a "fifty-fifty" chance that GHB was administered to Jeff during the night of his murder.

Kevin Conboy, one of Jeff's co-workers, would be called to testify at the re-sentencing trial. The prosecution wanted to reiterate the fact that Susan was overly concerned about Jeff's life insurance policy.

"It was clear that the conversation was about the insurance policy and whether or not Jeff had turned in the insurance policy," Conboy said. "That he would get it taken care of and he would turn in paperwork and he also said, 'If I die, you will be a very rich woman."

This go around, however, the defense team would make sure the jury knew about Susan's abuse. They would call on one of Jeff's brother-in-laws, Brian Roberts, who witnessed a fight between the couple.

"I saw her turn to Jeff with a knife," Roberts said.

He also claimed that he spoke to Susan about Jeff's abuse.

"I asked her if it had happened before."

"What was her answer?" the defense attorney asked.

"'Yes, 2,3,5 more than 6 times,' she said."

Kay Wright, Jeff's mother, would take the stand as well.

"He said, 'I love you, Mom'" Kay said, fighting back tears as she described her son's last words to her. She informed the jury that she had no reason to believe that Susan was lying when she said she kicked out Jeff during that fateful evening.

"I said, 'Has Jeff come back?' And she said, 'Yes he's come back.' And she said he got some of his clothes and he took my clothes and put bleach all over them in the bedroom and she also said he'd left a note that said thanks for betraying me or something like that. She said, 'If anything ever happens to me, I want my kids to live with my sister.' I said, 'Nothing is going to happen. Jeffrey will come home and we'll straighten this thing out."

Kay listened to all of this not knowing that her son Jeff lay dead, stabbed nearly 200 times just a few feet away from Susan.

But the defense had a better case this go around. The twenty-five-year punishment was reversed. Susan had been given leeway as she convinced the jury that she suffered from battered women syndrome.

"At the end of the day," Orange said. "This was an impulse murder. Susan had to tie Jeff down and most likely drug him up. Helpless and not knowing what else to do, she committed one of the most brutal murders I had ever studied. But she was not a psychopath. She was an abused woman who snapped and did something psychopathic. That doesn't mean that she shouldn't be duly punished. And it doesn't necessarily mean that she's a psychopath frothing at the mouth."

They would take off five years from Susan's sentence and make her eligible for parole.

"If we are to believe that Susan's allegations of abuse are true," Orange said. "Then she definitely was a poster child for battered women's syndrome. In other words, she could not leave Jeff whenever anyone looking at the situation objectively would. She acquired a learned state of helplessness. She lost hope at her ability to change the situation. There are some psychologists who believe that the battered woman can become homicidal when they are pushed to the brink. When Susan saw her son being hit by Jeff, she lost it."

Bradley and Kailey would later be adopted by Jeff's brother, Ronald.

HUSBAND KILLER : THE TRUE STORY OF AUDREY MARIE HILLEY

99

ANNA DELANEY

Audrey Marie Hilley

"That woman was pitiful," said Janice Hinds, 50, one of two neighbours who called police and cared for Hilley after spotting her sprawled on the deck of Thomason's home.

"We didn't know she was Marie Hilley. She didn't look like Marie Hilley," said Hinds, who grew up in the same Blue Mountain cotton-mill town as Hilley. "Marie Hilley was a sophisticated lady. She had pride in her looks, her dress."[1]

Her Early Life

Audrey Marie Hilley was born on June 4th, 1933 in Blue Mountain, Alabama. Her parents, Huey and Lucille Frazier, worked hard at the Linen Mill to provide for their family, and Marie (as she was known) was often looked after by relatives when her mother returned to work shortly after she was born.

Huey and Lucille loved their only child but showed their love with material things rather than affection and time. She was always well-dressed and had nice things, and as a result, Marie became rather spoilt. She was well known for her temper tantrums when things didn't go her way, and her parents, possibly out of guilt for not being there, rarely checked her for her behaviour.[2]

The Fraziers were proud people and were determined that their only child would not spend her life working in the same mills as they, and most of the town's inhabitants, had always done. They wanted more for their daughter and instilled in her an ambition to be a secretary, a lofty ambition for someone from a mill town.

In 1945, the Fraziers moved from Blue Mountain to Anniston, and Marie enrolled at Quintard Junior High School. Anniston was a whole new world to the girl who had felt she was above the rest in her old hometown. Marie went from being a big fish in a small pond to a small fish in a much more upscale lake, and for the first time in her life found herself at a disadvantage. In Anniston, all the girls wore nice dresses and what was more, some of their parents were the owners of the same mills that Marie's parents worked at.

Marie threw herself into her studies, making a name for herself as a diligent, intelligent student, and she integrated herself into new social circles – her friends were from privileged families and Marie wanted to be a part of that.

It wasn't just the teachers for whom Marie stood out, though. She was also a pretty girl and had her fair share of the attention from the boys, too. In fact, by the end of the 7th grade of Junior High School, Marie Hilley had been voted the prettiest girl in school by the yearbook staff.

It was around this time that 16-year-old Frank Hilley noticed 12-year-old Marie, and by the time he graduated High School, he was in love.[3]

Frank and Marie

In contrast to the Frazier family, who loved their daughter but showed no affection, Frank Hilley's family was warm and affectionate. The Hilleys worked in the other big industry of the area – pipe making - and even though they did not have much money, Clarence and Carrie Hilley made a happy, comfortable home for their three children – Frank, Jewel and Freeda.

Marie's parents did not approve of Frank – he was not from one of the affluent families of Anniston and Huey and Lucille wanted more for their daughter – but Marie was happy to be Frank's girl, and in return, he treated her like a princess.

Frank joined the Navy after finishing High School and was assigned to Guam but the distance between them bothered Frank. He was worried that with him so far away, and with so much time apart, Marie might find someone else so, on May 8th, 1951, before 17-year-old Marie had even finished High School, the young couple married.

Married Life

Marie remained in Anniston to finish her education and then joined Frank in Long Beach, California before the couple moved to Boston where Frank finished his stint in the Navy. It was while they were in Boston that they discovered Marie was pregnant with their first child, and the couple moved back to Anniston and bought a small home. Frank secured a job with a local foundry, and Marie found work as a secretary. Like all couples, the pair had their ups and downs, but for the most part, they seemed happy.

Their first child, Michael Hilley, was born on November 11th, 1952.

The Troubles Begin

Marie had been brought up to want the best of everything. While Frank was still in the Navy he had sent all of his paychecks home to his young wife, and yet when the time had come for her to join her new husband in California she had no money to pay for the journey. She had been spending his wages without telling him, and his parents had had to finance Marie's travel in order for her to join her new husband.

Despite the extra financial burdens having a young baby places on a family, Marie's spending didn't decrease. She wanted nice clothes and expensive home furnishings, and Frank, not liking to upset his wife, gave in to her, just as her parents had when she was a girl. Marie was a woman who was used to getting her own way.[4]

In 1959 Marie's behaviour began to become more sinister. She started taunting Frank, waving love letters she said were from other men in front of him but not letting him read them. She would then leave the torn up pieces where her husband could find them. Frank pieced them together, and it became clear that his wife had written them herself. When he confronted her she said she was afraid he didn't love her anymore and wanted to make him jealous.

By this time, Marie was spending double her take-home pay from her own job on fine clothes and luxuries. To prevent Frank, who was extremely responsible financially, from finding out she would get up early in the morning to check the mail and hide the bills.

Marie became pregnant again, and on January 14th, 1960 she gave birth to a baby daughter, whom they named Carol Marie.[5]

Carol

By the time Carol was born, things should have been looking up for the family. Frank had been promoted at work, and Marie had developed a reputation as a first class executive secretary. However, as the family's income rose, so did Marie's spending. Furthermore, she was becoming known for a peculiar situation at work. While her bosses loved her for her politeness and diligence, her co-workers greatly disliked her. They found her to be very judgemental of those around her and felt that she put on airs and graces and acted as if her co-workers were 'beneath' her. When she became disliked she would leave, and complain to friends and family that her colleagues had 'ganged up' on her and driven her from her job. Her employers, though, always gave her exemplary references, and she never found it difficult to get another job. In fact, Marie Hilley worked for some of the most powerful and affluent men in Anniston.[6]

Marie was disappointed with her daughter, Carol. She wanted her daughter to wear pretty dresses and have bows in her hair, while Carol was more of a tomboy and would often go to football games with her father. The pair developed a close father/daughter relationship and Marie was deeply resentful and jealous. She lamented the fact that her daughter was not feminine and demure and the pair argued constantly. Marie was much closer to her son, Mike, and like her parents before her never dished out discipline. Materially, the children wanted for nothing. Emotionally, it was a different story.

Going Up in the World

In 1962, Marie instigated a move to McClellan Boulevard, which was much closer to the houses of the affluent residents of Anniston that she so desperately tried to emulate. She felt that they were 'her' people. That same year, Marie's parents – Huey and Lucille moved in with the Hilleys.[7]

Marie's behaviour was becoming more and more out of control, and Frank was becoming increasingly concerned. He would often sit up with her during the night as she shook violently, unable to calm her. Perhaps the financial hole she had dug for the family was beginning to take its toll on Marie's psyche – by this time she had opened a Post Office Box and was having some of her bills sent there in order to avoid detection by Frank.

When the money ran out Marie started taking out loans. Frank was a well-respected man in the area and loans were secured against his good name and standing in the community. But creditors became concerned when bills and loan payment dates came and went without being settled, as Frank had always been a man who paid on time.[8]

On December 11th, 1965, Marie's father, Huey, died of cancer at the age of 57.[9]

In 1972, Mike graduated from High School and decided to pursue a career in the ministry, for which he went away to college.

Marie's behaviour towards her daughter, Carol, became more extreme. She often accused her of being a lesbian and would rant at Carol's female friends. Her paranoia at being found out in the lies regarding money must have been affecting her, because she also, around this time, stopped Frank from talking to his friends on the 'phone. It was also around this period of time that Frank Hilley became sick.[10]

Frank

During 1974 Frank had long periods of sickness. He put his frequent illnesses down to something he'd eaten, but soon the fatigue, vomiting and nausea could not be explained away by food. One day Frank came home from work early after succumbing to yet another bout of sickness, to find his wife in bed with her boss. His wife's spending suddenly made sense – she was sleeping with her employers for money. Frank was disgusted with his wife's behaviour but felt too ill and weak to deal with it. Instead, he turned to his son, Mike, who was by this time an ordained minister.[11]

However, that phone call, in which Frank arranged to meet Mike in Georgia where he now lived, was overheard by Audrey, who was listening in on an extension. From that moment on, Frank's symptoms worsened considerably, and he became seriously ill.[12]

On May 19th, 1975 Frank couldn't stand it any longer, and he consulted Dr Earl Jones, who diagnosed him initially with a viral stomach ache.[13] Dr Earl prescribed various medications, but nothing seemed to be helping. Frank's sister Freeda came to visit him, and he told her that he feared he was going to die, as he had never been so sick. He also told her that Marie had been administering him medicine via a syringe on the Dr's orders.[14]

On May 23rd, 1975, Frank was admitted to the Regional Medical Center. Tests indicated liver failure, and subsequently infectious hepatitis.[15] Frank was desperately ill, jaundiced and hallucinating. Mike, who had travelled to be with his father, had to restrain Frank from jumping out of the window. In the early hours of May 25th, Mike left the hospital to pick up his Grandmothers so that they could see Frank, but when he returned his mother was asleep and his father was dead. Frank Hilley was 45.[16]

Because of Frank's sudden death, an autopsy was performed, with Marie's blessing. Tests showed that Frank did indeed have hepatitis, along with swelling of the lungs and kidneys, inflammation of the stomach, and bilateral pneumonia.[17]

Life After Frank

With Frank's death being confirmed as being of natural causes, Marie made a claim on his life insurance and received a payment of

$31,140.[18] Marie went on a spending spree, indulging her love of luxury items. She bought new clothes, jewelery, and a new car. Her mother, Lucille, was still living with Marie and Carol and received a diamond ring. Carol herself was treated to numerous gifts, including a car and a stereo. It was hardly the behaviour of a grieving widow.[19]

In 1976 Mike and his then wife Teri moved in with the family. Shortly after Frank's death, Lucille had been diagnosed with cancer. Her health was failing and they were happy to help. However, it wasn't a good move for the young couple. Marie was restless, and often complained to anyone who would listen that nobody loved her, and would frequently complain about her boss and her job. She was highly dissatisfied with her life, and to make matters worse Marie and Carol fought endlessly, making family life fraught. Mike would often find himself torn between his mother, who would constantly demand his attention, and his wife, Teri, who had begun experiencing ill health since moving in with Marie. Hospitalised four times with illness, Teri also suffered a miscarriage, and the young couple decided to move out.

They found an apartment and were ready to move in, but the night before their move Marie's house caught fire. Mike and Teri moved into their apartment, with Marie, Carol and Lucille in tow. Repairs were soon made to Marie's house, but the night before his mother was due to go home, Mike's neighbour's apartment suffered the same fate and went up in flames. Mike and Teri had no choice but to move back in with Marie, Carol and Lucille. They were back where they began.[20]

A Strange Series of Events

Mike and Teri finally found their own home and moved away from Marie. On January 4th, 1977, Lucille lost her battle against widespread, aggressive cancer. Marie again came into money – a small sum of $600 from a burial policy.

Marie became well known to the local police. She was constantly reporting strange occurrences at her home. As well as petty thefts, she claimed that a fire had been started in her closet late one night. Coincidentally, Marie's neighbour, Doris Ford reported an almost identical fire in her own house (to which Marie had a key) the same night. There followed a succession of reports by both women of nuisance phone calls and other grievances.

Marie came up with many theories about where the harassment of both herself and her neighbour was coming from. She told Detective Gary Caroll that she suspected someone at the phone company of making the calls, as the calls seemed only to happen when the trace was taken off of her phone. She also claimed that one of her former employers had tried to force her to have sex and was harassing her because of her refusal. Yet another theory put forward by Marie was that, shortly after Frank's death, two men had arrived at her house demanding repayment of gambling debts.

When police put a trace on Doris Ford's phone, however, the calls were traced back to the Jenkins Manufacturing Plant, which just so happened to be where Marie was working.[21]

In 1978, Marie and Carol moved to Florida to live with Mike and Teri. Carol had just graduated, and Marie found herself a job in an office. Her out of control spending habits continued to cause problems when she ran up over $600 on Mike's credit card, promising to pay him back. This living arrangement only lasted a few short months, however, before Marie and Carol returned to Anniston.[22]

Mike and Teri were happy to see Marie leave. By that time they had a baby son called Joshua, and Mike feared that Marie would take the baby and disappear as she seemed to have an unhealthy fixation on him.[23]

Carol's Turn

Marie had no home of her own to return to when she and Carol moved back to Anniston. At first, they stayed with Freeda, Frank's sister, and then they moved in with Carrie Hilley, Frank's mother.

Once they were settled at Carrie's house, the strange happenings recommenced. Items went missing, phone lines were cut, and small fires were started. Illness also struck the household – Carrie Hilley started suffering from nausea and vomiting.

Marie started a new job, and very quickly started an affair with her boss, Harold Dillard, and began manipulating him to leave his wife. At the same time, she also started seeing Calvin Robertson, an old school friend. Calvin believed Marie when she told him she had cancer and needed expensive treatment, and he gladly gave her the money for the 'fictitious' illness. When Marie told him some time later that she was now cancer-free he was elated, and so smitten that he would have done anything for her.

It was also during this time that Marie began buying insurance policies. Not only did she take out fire insurance, cancer insurance, and her own life insurance, she also took out insurance policies on the lives of her two children. Mike was insured for $25,000 while Carol had two policies on her life, totalling $39,000.

Carol's senior prom came in April 1979. During the evening Carol started to feel ill. It wasn't enough to make her leave the party, though, so she ignored her symptoms. The next day, however, she was so ill during a church service that she had to leave the service early and vomited in the car park. Coincidentally, Carrie Hilley had also taken ill at church and was taken to hospital after fainting.[24]

By August 1979 Carol had been admitted to the Emergency Room several times with nausea and vomiting. After yet another episode of sickness in August, Marie gave her daughter an injection into her hip, which she said would ease the nausea. Instead of easing, however, Carol's illness took a serious downturn. Not only did the injection not ease Carol's sickness, it also caused her fingers and legs to become numb and weak.

On August 22nd, 1979 she was admitted to the Anniston Hospital by Dr Warren Sarrell. When, by August 29th Dr Sarrell had been unable to find a cause for Carol's symptoms, he sent her for a psychiatric evaluation at the Carraway Methodist Hospital in Birmingham. While under the care of Dr John Elmore, Carol was given two further injections by her mother – injections which, she was told, would help with her weak legs. She told Carol that the injections had been supplied by Doris Ford, who was a registered nurse, and that Carol could tell no-one as Doris would get into trouble if she was found out.

On September 18th, 1979, with Carol still in the hospital, Marie asked Dr Elmore what was wrong with her daughter. He told her that she was suffering from vitamin deficiencies and malnutrition, and, in his opinion, lead poisoning. Carol took exception to this diagnosis and, against Dr Elmore's advice, discharged Carol from the hospital.

On September 19th, Carol was once again admitted to the hospital, this time to the University of Alabama Hospital in Birmingham. The same day, Marie was arrested as her fraudulent ways finally caught up with her. Her arrest was what, ultimately, saved Carol's life. Marie was taken in for questioning, and Carol was examined by Dr Brian Thompson, who noticed that, along with the numbness in her hands and feet, Carol also had striations on her nails, called Aldridge Mee's Lines. He explained that these markings were typical of arsenic poisoning, and ordered tests on Carol's hair.

The initial findings revealed that Carol had over 50 times the normal arsenic level of human hair. Shockingly, when more detailed tests were carried out on October 3rd, 1979 they showed that the hair close to Carol's scalp had over 100 times the normal levels, while hair further down the hair shaft the levels were lower, right down to zero at the ends. This indicated, according to Forensic Scientist John Case, that Carol had been systematically poisoned with arsenic over a period of four to eight months, with the dosages given in increasingly higher strengths.

Furthermore, with Marie unable to be with her daughter, Carol's conditioned improved dramatically during her time at the hospital.[25]

On the strength of these findings, Frank Hilley's body was exhumed, and once again large levels of arsenic were found. His cause of death was changed to that of arsenic poisoning. The same substance was also discovered to have been present in both Lucille Frazier and Carrie Hilley (who had died recently) at the time of their deaths, although not fatal amounts.[26]

On October 9th, 1979, while still incarcerated for the fraudulent charges, Marie Hilley was arrested for the attempted murder of Carol. As part of their ongoing, and increasingly serious, investigations the Anniston police found a vial in Marie's purse – a vial which testing confirmed contained arsenic.

On November 9th, 1979, Marie made bail and was released, under the name of Emily Stephens, to a local motel. However, Marie was not going to just sit and await her trial, and somewhere between October 9th and October 18th, Marie disappeared. A note was found in her motel room, suggesting that she 'might' have been kidnapped.

Audrey Marie Hilley was now a fugitive and would remain so for more than three years.[27]

A New Identity

There were only a few clues for the police to go on after Marie disappeared. Margaret Key, Marie's Aunt, reported that her home had been broken into and that her car and some clothes had disappeared. The police called in the FBI, but once the car was found abandoned in Georgia the trail went cold very quickly.

On January 11th, 1980, Marie Hilley, still a fugitive, was indicted for the murder of her husband, Frank Hilley.

Marie, meanwhile, had assumed a new identity in Florida. Robbi Hannon, as she was now known, was working her charm on a man called John Homan. Robbi told John tales of her imaginary tragic past, and John, who hadn't had the easiest of lives himself, fell for both the stories and for Robbi. She told him that she had lost her children in a car accident and John felt as though he had found a kindred spirit.

He fell in love, hook, line, and sinker.

On May 29th, 1981 Robbi and John were married, after which they moved to Marlow, New Hampshire. They both found work there and rented a house. Robbi's new job was in customer service at the Central Screw Corporation, where she excelled. The men found her to be fun, while her co-workers, for the most part, found her pleasant, although a few took a dislike to her. She regaled the staff with stories of a wealthy family in Texas, whose fortune she would inherit one day, and garnered sympathy by telling them about her two children dying in a car accident.

She would also talk of an identical twin sister called Teri Martin, who lived in Texas, making frequent reference to her.

Robbi would, from time to time, complain of searing headaches, and told John that she was seeking treatment from specialists. Until one day, Robbi came to John and told him it had been discovered that she was suffering from an incurable blood disease. It was her twin sister, Teri, who would be looking after Robbi when she made one last trip to Texas in search of a cure, and in September 1982, Robbi left Marlow to seek treatment.

Of course, there was no incurable disease, and no twin sister, either. Robbi only stayed in Texas for a few days, and then made her way to Florida, where she bleached her hair blond, and found work as a secretary, using the name Teri Martin. During her six weeks at her new job, Teri confided in her boss, Jack McKenzie, about her terminally ill twin sister Robbie. In early November, Teri called Jack and told him Robbi had died, and that she was needed in New Hampshire.

On November 10th, 'Teri' called John Homan and told him his wife had died, and the following day she flew back to New Hampshire.

During her time away, 'Teri' had lost a lot of weight, and changed her hair color to blond, so John easily accepted that this was his dead wife's twin sister. The pair went to the local paper and placed an obituary for Robbi, and then John took Teri to his wife's workplace – The Central Screw Corporation – and introduced the workers to Robbi's twin sister. While some of the staff accepted Teri's appearance, some did not and were highly suspicious.

Teri insisted on moving in with John Homan, saying they needed to help each other grieve, and she found herself a job as a secretary at a book printing company.

Meanwhile, the suspicions were still rising at Robbi's old workplace, and a few of the doubters decided to take a closer look into Robbi's obituary. Their suspicions were confirmed when they discovered that the details mentioned in the paper were fictitious, and they took those suspicions to the police.

Arrested

On January 12th, 1983, the police apprehended Teri at work. They had been watching her and thought she might be another fugitive, Terry Lynn Clifton. However, when they asked her her name she told them it was Audrey Marie Hilley, and that she was wanted for fraud. The local police ran a check on her name and discovered that she was wanted for much more than bad checks.

On January 19th, 1983, Marie was brought back to Anniston. Carol was desperate to see her mother, to find some answers, but although Marie professed her love for her daughter she gave no explanation for the poisoning. Prosecutors were worried that Carol's love for her mother would go in Marie's favour and that Carol would not say anything against her mother.

They needn't have worried.

Carol's testimony about her mother giving her the injections was solid. Marie had told her attorneys that after her arrest in 1979 she had been interviewed but she failed to mention that that interview had been recorded. During that interview, Marie admitted to giving Carol the injections and the recording was there for all to hear. Carol's defense fell apart.

The jury needed only three hours to return their verdicts – guilty of the murder of Frank Hilley, and of the attempted murder of Carol Hilley.

Judge Sam Monk sentenced Marie to life imprisonment for Frank's murder, plus twenty years for the poisonings, and on June 9th, 1983, Marie was taken to Tutwiler State Women's Prison in Wetumpka, Alabama.

Marie's Escape

Marie was a perfect prisoner. She never caused trouble and was classified as a minimum security prisoner. This classification meant that she was eligible for leave from the prison. Between late 1986 and February 1987, Marie had left prison for eight hours on four occasions, returning on time with each leave.

On February 19th, 1987, Marie left the prison on a three-day leave pass. John had, by this time, moved to Anniston so that he and his wife could spend her leave together whenever they could.

On February 22nd, Marie arranged to meet John at her parents' graves. Marie never showed up, and John found, instead, a note from his wife.

"I hope you will be able to forgive me," it read. *"I'm getting ready to leave. It will be best for everybody. We'll be together again. Please give me an hour to get out of town."*

John took the note to the police, and, given Marie's past cunning, they assumed she was already far out of state, and started, once again, searching for her.[28]

Her Death

Marie hadn't gone far. On February 26th, 1987, Aniston police received a phone call. Marie had been found huddled behind a house, apparently having wandered in the woods for four days. The weather had been terrible – heavy rain and low temperatures – and Marie was suffering from hypothermia and delirium. Marie started having convulsions, and, in the ambulance on the way to the hospital, Audrey Marie Hilley took her last breath.

On February 28th, 1987, Marie was buried next to her husband, Frank, at their children's request.[29] Her second husband, John Homan, died two years later in 1989 while working as a caretaker in Anniston. He intervened in a fight and was stabbed to death. Marie's note to John, in which she said that they would be together again, had come true a lot sooner than anyone would have predicted.[30]